The Great Sacrifice of Jesus the Christ

by
Ahmed Ismail

Trafford
PUBLISHING®

Order this book online at www.trafford.com/08-1041
or email orders@trafford.com

Most Trafford titles are also available at major online book retailers.

Cover Design: Luqman Nagy.

Note for Librarians: A cataloguing record for this book is available from Library
and Archives Canada at www.collectionscanada.ca/amicus/index-e.html

ISBN: 978-1-4251-8531-2

*We at Trafford believe that it is the responsibility of us all, as both individuals
and corporations, to make choices that are environmentally and socially sound.
You, in turn, are supporting this responsible conduct each time you purchase a
Trafford book, or make use of our publishing services. To find out how you are
helping, please visit www.trafford.com/responsiblepublishing.html*

*Our mission is to efficiently provide the world's finest, most comprehensive
book publishing service, enabling every author to experience success.
To find out how to publish your book, your way, and have it available
worldwide, visit us online at www.trafford.com/10510*

Trafford PUBLISHING® www.trafford.com

North America & international
toll-free: 1 888 232 4444 (USA & Canada)
phone: 250 383 6864 ♦ fax: 250 383 6804 ♦ email: info@trafford.com

The United Kingdom & Europe
phone: +44 (0)1865 487 395 ♦ local rate: 0845 230 9601
facsimile: +44 (0)1865 481 507 ♦ email: info.uk@trafford.com

10 9 8 7 6 5 4 3

CONTENTS

INTRODUCTION

Quite a bit of my last four books were 'inspired' by a single verse in the Quran. That verse is as follows:

Verily, the likeness of Jesus before Allah is the likeness of Adam. He created him from dust, then (He) said to him: "Be" and he was. Q (3: 59) (1, 37)

This may cause some consternation in some circles but it is absolutely true. And many more books could be written about that verse but who has the capacity to do that? So all praise is due to the Creator Lord Who made us alive and gave us both depth and simplicity from Himself.

The creation of Jesus (pbh) as a 'new creation' is easy enough to understand when viewed in a certain light. He, as a man of God, certainly deserves our respect and why not? Didn't he **"pour forth his soul unto death …"** as the great prophet Isaiah declared? He most certainly did!

Although he didn't die, such that he was **not crucified**

nor was he put to death, (2) but rather was raised up to the heavens in body and soul to return one day to lead the faithful in the paradise on Earth for the Promise made by the One God must be carried out (3, 41). Then he shall die and be buried alongside the Prophet (pbh) from whence they will raise together on the Last Day of Judgment (4, 5).

But why does the Prophet (pbh) love the man Jesus (pbh) so much and why the placement of their bodies so close to each other when Jesus will die the death of the normal man (6)? Why?

Like Isaiah (pbh) said and that is why. And he said, "he poured out his soul unto death …" That is also why he is known not only as Jesus but is called Jesus the Christ.

This seems like a complex issue but the scriptures tell the story or as much of it as we can be aware of provided of course that the scriptures are read correctly and not taken as common fodder or treated like a comic book. Worse than that is the treatment of the scriptures as our own property to make them to say what we want them to say. Yes, there has been some jiggling of the 'facts' as presented. For example, Matthew (27: 46) (7) and Luke (23:43) (8) are not technically wrong according to Islamic science. No, they are not wrong but they are taken out of place to fashion a peculiar story that did not happen as people have been led to believe happened.

And this is the puzzler. How is it that when the history of these scriptures are taken into account along with the history of men's souls and the evils that have arisen so abundantly throughout history, how is it that there remain any scriptures at all?

Man's power of evil eradication combined with his carelessness would have seemed to be enough to eradicate the scriptures and to even throw down the foundations of the heavens. Foolish man, did he think that he was that powerful? He may have been that vain but definitely he is not the one in charge. (9)

For example, the true history of the Old and New Testaments and their formation gives one a chance to reflect. When one considers that several times the Old Testament seems to have disappeared at various times gives one a chance to ponder.

It is not that they are completely pure but that they exist at all in a goodly form cannot be a testimony to mankind's goodness. What mankind does with them is another thing altogether. Such is the power of the One God's Plan that the puny storms stirred up by man could not quench the truth. For if man is guided rightly, then he is guided by stages hidden from his knowledge but not from the One Who created him with His hands and breathed into him something of His spirit.

Along with this intriguing puzzle are the questions of the 'soul' and that of 'sin'. Of the two, the idea of sin is a lot easier to grasp yet that also remains very hard to fathom due to its complexity. Yet that knowledge does not have to be known because it changes nothing that is real. In the most simplistic sense, which is often the best way to look at things, one can say, "the soul is the soul and sin is sin so let us leave it at that." That idea coupled with faith is enough but some have come to feed off the meat as uninvited guests causing havoc among the unwary.

So what would one do if he saw a hungry wolf breaking into a friend's house while the friend was sleeping? Would one feel comfortable to 'let nature take its course'? After all, the hungry wolf did not come to our door so why should we risk anything? Perhaps the wolf may eat our 'friend' but then he should be well satiated and will leave us alone. That is one way of looking at it until the shoe is on the other foot.

Then there is the story of The Wall. This is not the story

of the Berlin Wall or the Wall put up recently in Palestine although the idea of both walls comes from 'kindred spirits' or similar groups hell-bent on achieving the same malicious goals. No, this is a story about what is affectionately called in some quarters as 'The Wall'.

Now one would think that The Wall would be gristle for the mill of the scientific mind. Having been brought up short (just a little bit anyway) in two of my other books – *He Is Not My Ancestor* and *The Real Holy Grail: The Messiah on Trial* – some of the scientific persuasion will not be amused. In fact, due to the severity of the issue, some may wish that The Wall would be only a figment of a fertile imagination to use kind words.

However, it does exist physically and a primitive extension of its 'roots' has been photographed many times.

The Wall if put under a true scientific enquiry, would do no less than shake the senses of the world – scientific or otherwise. And the problem just won't dry up and go away much to the amusement of some and the consternation of others.

And of course there always seems to be that titillating subject of flying saucers to go around which has infected close to a billion people in various ways. It would be funny if it didn't lead some to try and get away from the 'Word' of Life and expect great things from the so-called superior race of little green men. The answer to that is stuff and nonsense! Yes, these objects are real enough – just as real as a tree but one shouldn't be misled into strange and fanciful beliefs like one would lead a dog on a collar.

References in this book will be shown mostly in the special section dealing with such things and numbers will be placed in parenthesis where the reader will be directed to go to such references.

THE SACRIFICE MOST HOLY

It has been stated in scripture that God created the heavens and earths in 6 days. In fact, He created all the universe of what can be seen and what cannot be seen in 6 days. Then?

Well He did not rest or sleep but this creation had been fashioned to evolve in complete perfection. All potential avenues of expression (that what came into being and those forces commanding the laws that hold all things together) in fact, all things and all pathways of infinite development were molded into His creation and nothing was that ever came forth was not unaccounted for. Nothing that could occur or that could ever occur in any phase or development was overlooked.

Indeed! It was a totally perfect and controlled system with infinite systems found within infinite systems – self perpetuating and evolving according to His Designed Plan. Man can barely begin to comprehend His Designs or even the grand scale of time as countless processes evolved and came into being.

But He Who created these things set it as His footstool in perfect harmony and even what would appear to us fragile humans as chaos was planned down to the smallest of details – planned with total perfection.

The AL-Bari – one of His Holy Names means in part The Evolver – and while the system continued to expand and grow such as we now know from the science of astronomy, there came the creations of the Angels out of Light and the Jinn out of smokeless fire and things were set down for them also. And they were overawed by the complexity of things and could not comprehend the Mind that unleashed this magnificent creation which was so far above their comprehension but easy to accomplish by Him Who made all things.

The Jinn, just like mankind would do in the future, had the ability to sense the awe and wonder of this complex system of creation called the universe which unbeknown to them was such a simple thing for their Lord to create. This universe, which is nothing more than His footstool, defined here as a creation that is at His Feet and totally under His control, has been admired by man for ages. In fact, until recently most scientists didn't know much about the universe at all. Now we are in a position to say a few things of which I believe are some things that are correct and some things that are plain silly.

It appears from scientific study that this universe, according to scientists anyway, should last about forty billion or so years before it winks out of existence. That thought comes from extensive studies based on gravity, the speed of the galaxies racing away from each other, star life and a whole host of other things.

Those are logical thoughts to be sure. However, according to Prophet Muhammad (pbh) this universe with its almost unimaginable distances and countless galaxies filled with innumerable stars is only His footstool. That footstool has been compared by the Prophet (pbh) to being just like a 'ring' thrown out in the empty space of the desert. It is a ring with a lot of bright specks in it representing the galaxies but a simple ring nonetheless. This ring is called in Arabic Al-Kursi or the footstool (10).

Now we all know that Prophet Muhammad (pbh) didn't come to teach theoretical physics 101 but the amazing thing is that when we take a closer look at this ring with an understanding of science some amazing things happen.

Theoretically, if a man were to take a spacecraft and starting at point X, what would happen if he continued his journey to the end of the universe? He would end up where he began and that is point X. So, he would loop himself around to the position he started at. Hence, one can understand the idea of the universe being likened unto a ring. Mankind, if given the power by Allah, can indeed visit this heaven and actually as most of us know, we have been to the Moon and spacecraft have visited various parts of the solar system.

The real Big News is not the humble footstool which man has been placed in but the 'Arsh that the Prophet talked about. This is the place of His Throne which is placed above an immense sea which is above the various levels of the seven heavens. This is the REAL place of excellent dignity but of which we know practically nothing about even through Divine Revelation.

Why is this important? It would be important for many reasons but one of them can stand out to make an example of mankind's dependency on His Creator Lord as well as all life must. Such thoughts can hardly be put into words but at least one can try.

Think of a curtain or veil being placed in between the Kursi and the 'Arsh. A veil one can never cross in this our normal state of existence. Not only can it not be crossed or sensed or even seen but a barrier nonetheless. And because our senses and our minds are limited to the wonders of this footstool, we are unaware of the presence of that veil.

So have a friend draw some pinpoints representing the myriad number of galaxies containing countless stars on a piece of paper while you stand behind a curtain that has an <u>invisible</u> slit running through it. Let your friend stand close to that slit while holding up that paper image of the 'infinite' universe we call home.

Now in the twinkling of an eye reach out and grab that piece of paper and crush it up in your hands folding up our pretend universe as if it was nothing but mere paper which of course it was in this experiment. A humbling experience to be sure!

This very crude example was offered to show several things. First, no doubt that if the universe was creating itself or bringing itself into existence, the scientists have an inside track on about how long it will last. Obviously, the universe's creation (the big bang theory) did not create itself. Even though it runs on what can be called timely laws, it does not have a brain to control itself. It is tended and cared for by what has been put in place, commonly called laws and other things so that there is a sense of rhythm to it. But one must not forget Who created it and how easy that was for Him to do. Moreover, He is the One in charge and He is He Who does what He Wills and He cannot be questioned about it. Under this idea then, He is the One Who can dispose of it <u>when and how</u> He likes and that is also easy for Him to do – as and when He Wills (11).

Is this frightening? Not really for those who have faith and know where to go to depend on the One Who is the Real Giver of Life. The above example just puts things in a more proper perspective giving some an idea to show more thoughtfulness and less arrogance. Furthermore, it gives man a real chance to pause and reflect on his own creation and dependency on Him Who is the Originator of all things.

Some foolish people have been known to try and guess where this 'Arsh of Allah might be located by studying certain hadith material. Furthermore, some foolish people might wonder that if there is a huge sea floating around in the sky, then why doesn't it slosh around and spill over or why can't it be seen? The 'Arsh is not of this lowly but vast universe to begin with and whether the 'veil' is before the Moon or after it is nobody's business at all. How could something like that be known anyway?

Therefore, it is better to leave off that which cannot be known and stay with the attempt of trying to understand that which can be known or that which is practical to be known. For the 'Arsh is just that unknowable but existing Throne from whence Allah Reigns in Power and as for His Essence or Being, He has given us only what He has chosen to give us of the knowledge of Himself. This should put man in the mind frame of being humbled in spirit and to become aware that no matter how man's exploits at times seem great such that one man might raise the dead or that another might crack the Moon in half which the Prophet did; man is still only a part of the vast creation that we can see and not as magnificent as some have declared.

With the creation of this universe and the Angels and Jinn some must have seen or sensed a feeling of Sacrifice as even the stars that die do so that others may be born.

And time past and a new creation appeared – a simple thing was made by His Command and a lot less complicated than the universe. A creature out of sounding clay was fashioned and brought up to where it was to be placed. It was a dead thing as of yet and in due time it would receive the gift of life by having a 'spirit' breathed into it but for now it remained lifeless (12). And many Angels and Jinn marveled at it but it was not a living thing and its purpose remained unknown. It was a common, very common thing fashioned with excellence but still a very simple, common thing being made from essentially water and clay.

That thing was known as Adam but it was still not yet a living thing. And one creature from amongst the Jinn, a creature called Iblis whose snooping abilities had gained him much knowledge, became curious about Adam's standing in things to come for if it (Adam) was to get life, it most assuredly would have a place in the grand but unknown scheme of things.

This Iblis entity would later become known as the evil father of perdition or the Satan due to his pride and arrogance he developed in his self-assurance and disobedience to his Lord. However, for now he was just curious about this statuesque sculptured piece of clay. After all, it might turn to his advantage to have a lowly species of creature that he might get enjoyment from by giving it lectures.

And seeing the hallow space in its back, he thought less of that creation and knew not its purpose. In truth, Iblis was a powerful entity who did serve his Creator Lord but he was moving ever closer to crossing the line that should never be crossed. He was in fact becoming infatuated with himself.

When the lifeless Adam was given life and the Angels and Jinn were told to <u>bow down</u> to this clay-like creature some rumblings arose. The soon to be evil one knew many things about the physical universe of which some things were beneath his mighty powers. And he knew the corruptions of the physical world as the physical life degenerates and carries out bodily functions.

To bow down to this inferior being of plain mud and water no matter what stature given to it didn't make any sense. And why should this contemptible piece of clay no matter what gifts it would be given be lifted to a higher station than one made of smokeless fire and imbued with great intellect? (13)

Does one find a modern day world leader voluntarily joining a leper colony to serve its inmates? So why should this mighty being (Iblis) obey his Creator and bow down to this piece of abject clay?

The rest of the story is history. And unlike the father of perdition who forgot that Allah was The Aware, The Most Powerful, many of his kind (Jinn creatures) did fear lest they be sent to their ruin.

But Adam was not created without a purpose. Although he did not know it at the time, he was born to learn the meaning of the word Sacrifice and what that was to entail – for he was not created by the very hands of Allah and raised up in a splendorous position without a Plan.

Although Adam did not know what that Plan would be, he did learn what the word Sacrifice was to be and how gut-wrenching it was to accomplish (14).

And down through the ages humanity has had to make sacrifices to deem themselves worthy of what was by birthright theirs if they chose to do it – for that is the test put on their shoulders but not on anyone else's (9, 15, 16).

And the Plan evolves like the phases of the Moon going forward as He designed it right down to the last atom in perfection. Perfection to perfection in measured parts just as He designed it. Of that matter, none knows much but all (save the Angelic slaves) have a share in contributing or trying to oppose His Plan.

The opposition always loses even when they seemingly win but unable to control anything like time, place, position or condition (except in the corrupt fantasies of the mind) they are ultimately and totally defeated. As these woe-forlorn creatures (both men and Jinn) try their best at sabotage, they are continually outflanked and outgunned by the very forces they are trying to defeat. Worse yet for them is that they are unaware of the records being kept to condemn them when they will face Reality (17, 18).

And these records are written by trustworthy hands but they are outsourced from the very 'souls' that would try to hide them in the end. In other words, it is by their own hands or what has passed from them that they daringly go forth to imbibe in spiritual suicide (19).

Like the phases of the Moon, the Sacrifice changes.

It wasn't so long ago in geological time that a mighty man who was to become known as the Friend of God was put under great stress to sacrifice his first-born son (his only son up to that time for his wife was barren). Before this the Sacrifice of Abel, Noah and others meant death in some form.

But something <u>changed</u> even though death can be said to be a part of the great Sacrifice.

The story of Abraham (pbh) the Friend of God is quite a story. He underwent many trials and tribulations in his life but was given great news of peoples to populate a great region called in the modern parlance the Middle East. The Middle East is where the People of the Book were to spring from. It would be the eventual fountainhead of three great religious movements and the birth place of the Lawgiver, the Messiah and the Messenger of messengers.

Like all things born on Earth, there would be no free ride and as much Light would enter the world, there would appear darkness and the intense story of the sons of light versus the sons of darkness continues to this very day.

O there are other ways and lessons to be learned but no man is in charge of that. The important thing is that the Way, with all of its implications both from the past going all the way back to the valley of Bakkah (now known as Makkah) to the future of the kingdom of the 5th Age whose center is in Jerusalem known before as Salem one would find a physical as well as spiritual setting. That represents a lot of historical past and a lot for the history of the future.

Even the Anti-christ that foul criminal finger of Satan will be given his short dominion of sorts showing the dark dreaded power of a vicegerent gone evil. But enough about his very brief but deadly rampage for the lands of blessedness will be washed clean of his filth and that mindless degenerate swarm (Gog and Magog) that will come after him.

This land is worth fighting for and maintained and history shows who best made things better for the people in a religious sense. No matter, for all of that is locked up and kept in safely guarded records.

The importance of this area and its celebration of faith and the Promise to come for mankind **who would accept it** were immense. It was an honor bestowed out of Love by no less than the Creator Lord Himself to His Friend Abraham (pbh) who had enjoyed his Lord's Protection and Goodwill.

But something terrible had seemingly happened! The loyal and old prophet, whose seed was to be as numerous as the stars, was shaken to his very foundation. His joy turned to sadness – a depth of sadness that penetrated through his very bones and squeezed his heart in an unbelievable grip.

Being both old and with a barren wife was all right because he had taken another wife who bore him his first born from whence in the future they were to do service to their Lord and were further honored in rebuilding the Kabbah in Makkah as a reborn place of honor stretching all the way back to Adam thus providing a great lineage.

But why must he now be ordered to destroy that which he loved above even himself? And if his first born should perish and the dream of the blessed nations by rejected, could it be that he, (God's Friend) had committed some unspeakable crime or was he to be rejected as unworthy?

Always obedient to his Lord's Call, he moved with his very

young son up a hill to do the deed that must be accomplished. But he moved with a terrible weight on his shoulders and his heart was sorely being squeezed such that death itself would be a great release. Yet his Lord must be obeyed. And even when his son encouraged him to move forward to carry out his task, Friend Abraham (pbh) felt stricken and in near despair but his duty was clear and his love for Allah so great that any selfish pride he may have felt in moments of past joy was burned out of his heart.

Before he could sacrifice his first born son, Allah granted to him and symbolically to the world, if they but would have it, a **Substitute** ram from heaven. Thus, Abraham filled with joy overcame the test and together with his son participated in the Sacrifice of monumental import (20).

And for this reason was Abraham (pbh) given the joy of the Great News (21, 22, and 23). Furthermore, he was given another piece of Great News which was that he would author another son, another holy child of great import, even a son from his barren wife: a child of destiny (as was his first son) but who would go on to form a line of greatness filled with many prophets culminating in the one prophet who would be That Sacrifice and known in history as the Messiah.

Now Abraham (pbh) was given two mighty gifts from his household and the man is given dominion over such things and is honored by his Lord as to have it become his household and the name of his children following after his name. His line would eventually lead to the birth of the Messenger of Allah (Muhammad) and a line also would be given that would lead to the birth of the Messiah known as Jesus the son of Mary – each line according to His Plan for the Salvation that has yet to come. But a PROMISE from the Creator Lord is a PROMISE that will not be defeated nor made undone.

So in part this is the story of Abraham (pbh) the <u>father of the prophets</u>. Like a true evolutionary force, the Promise would continue to move through history at the correct tempo and time as had been planned from beforehand.

And the evolution continued for the state of promise looked fairly bleak and particularly invisible at times especially with the degenerates like pharaoh on the scene. But once again the Light would shine brightly as His Plan poured forth in strength and power (24).

Born into the world came a mighty messenger called Moses (pbh) and from his trials, tribulations and sacrifice once again the Light shone brightly. And for his unquenchable determination would spring a whole host of prophets renewing the faith and giving guidance that was straight and true.

As many people, however, grew in excellence and purity, many more turned into backstabbers and backsliders thus causing great carnage to their peoples. This we get from their own records not to mention the records sent after them.

Once again, those who strove against the Light far outnumbered the ones who lived in the Light and no amount of prophets sent to them would turn their hearts to Him Who gives Life. So history moved on and those who lived in honor died in honor and those who lived in dishonor died in dishonor and never were a people so set upon and yet have their line continue. But they were warned repeatedly by their prophets of old not to continue in their old ways of disobedience for Allah supports not thankless peoples (25).

The end was drawing near. The old skin was about to be changed for the new for The Promise to start the unlocking of Salvation drew nigh. For born to the world was an epic birth of a holy child – a new creation which the gates of Hell itself could not withstand – for those who would choose it that is (26).

Required from him would be a monumental Sacrifice. A Sign that man's destiny would not continue unabated but that it would soon be fulfilled. Up until his birth, as far as anyone could guess, a million years might pass before mankind could inherit the Promise of eternal life or death as the case might be in the two abodes of home (Hell and Paradise) as promised from the 'fathers'.

The question is how could Judgment come before its time? Man does not set the time. Allah sets the time and the conditions. And this is not done by random chance. Therefore, Prophet Muhammad (pbh) would not be born before Moses (pbh) but must enter into the world when he is supposed to come. Yet all things have their order and he cannot come with the purified Way before the way is purified. That would be like building and setting the roof of a house in place before the walls were put up!

So, into the world was born a special child. A special child that would prepare the way for Allah's Messenger and become a Sign unto mankind. A special child who would be born into purity but undergo a great Sacrifice to become Pure so that purity could beget purity (27).

The Story Begins

Actually the story begins at some unknown place and time. However, for our intent and purpose the story of the great Sacrifice of Jesus the son of Mary (pbh) is mentioned in the book of Isaiah. Isaiah (pbh) was a true prophet from the Lord Most High. It is in his writings that declare that a certain death will come upon the Messiah. And that this 'death' will have certain consequences.

Several worthy Muslim investigators including the late Ahmed Deedat and Dr. Jamal Badawi to name just a few have familiarized themselves and discussed the records from the People of the Book. Among these records is a well respected book called Isaiah.

In this book there are many chapters and this book does discuss topics such as the Arabs, Prophet Muhammad (pbh), Islam, Caliph 'Umar and the Messiah to name just a few items.

One of the most famous phrases taken from this book is **"and he poured out his soul unto death ..."** found in Isaiah (53: 12), (28). Is there a problem with this? Apparently there is with some and the problem seems to lie in the context of the meaning. But to be sure, the saying, "and he poured out his soul unto death" is correct.

Some possibilities seem to arise among the various groups depending on the philosophical slant one wishes to put on things and how a judgment of this would affect things.

Some of the possibilities are as follows:
1. The Isaiah text has in this context been corrupted.
2. The original language in this phrase has been altered.
3. There is a problem with translation from the original language to that what is currently found.
4. Isaiah was lying (God forbid)
5. The language he used can only mean one thing because everybody knows what death means and it only has one connotation. Therefore, the Messiah died on the cross no matter what anybody says.

6. Isaiah (pbh) was telling the truth but most people do not understand what he meant.

These six possibilities are intriguing and each one no doubt will have its supporters. Frankly speaking, the findings of the Dead Sea Scrolls with the now famous 'copper scroll' of Isaiah should put to rest a lot of conjectures concerning his famous Chapter 53.

Because Holy Scripture is not regulated to the level of a comic book or surrendered to private (willy-nilly) interpretations, but rather should be harmonized with all true scripture, one is forced to conclude that some 'death' took place even unto his pouring out his soul unto death'.

In my last book, *The Non-Crucifixion of Jesus*, I was quick to point out that Jesus (pbh) did not die and was not even put on the cross. Is there a problem here? Not according to the records and the understanding of such. In fact with the proper understanding of the records the phrase "and he poured out his soul unto death" becomes understandable.

What could the possible interpretation for this partial verse be? Based on all the known evidence including the corrupted form of the *Epistle to the Hebrews* which discusses these things, the idea of death takes on a new meaning besides the physical death. (See appendix A for a discussion concerning the *Epistle to the Hebrews*.)

To suggest that a full understanding of the term death or sin based on what is found in Isaiah (pbh) can be completely known is unwarranted, foolish and absolutely wrong. Only a partial explanation can one hope to obtain but that should be quite enough. With this idea and the understanding of treating the other scriptures with respect, it is possible to feel more awareness concerning the great Sacrifice of Jesus the son of Mary (pbh).

Unfortunately, some find it 'fun' to delve into flights of fantasy or use a certain type of circular reasoning peculiar to the human mind.

Fortunately, there is a Standard by which judgment becomes clearer in the hunt for the truth. This Standard (29), which is accepted by some and rejected by others, is the Quran and the Sunnah of Prophet Muhammad (pbh) and this can be explained further from the various scriptures especially in the critical but special relationship between the Prophet and the Messiah as expressed in Holy Scripture including Isaiah.

The evolution of religion is a Planned evolution and not a lucky stab in the dark or some primitive voodoo rite carried over from the dark superstitious era of primitive primates who fashioned fables of their creation. It is Allah Who is in total control but most men are unaware.

Some might say that these matters are too complicated to understand. They are very complex to be sure but beginnings of understanding can be reached through various methods to attempt to make the complex less complex as long as the records remain in tact and the records cannot be broken!

In a discussion concerning the New Testament and the topic of death Mr. Ahmed Deedat has pointed out that Paul in one of his epistles declares something to the effect that 'every day he dies'. If one was to take that statement literally, it would be a very peculiar thing for Paul to physically die every day and still be found eating and drinking among the living. So obviously death has a peculiar meaning in Paul's vernacular in the context that he was using.

The next item on the agenda is especially hard to delve into without having an understanding of several scriptures. But since most people are not in a position for that an analogy must be applied.

The soul of man is not very well understood. In fact, it remains a mystery. But what forms part of the soul and sometimes used as an expression for the soul is the term (nefs) in Arabic. If one were to lose one's nefs, basically one can be said to be <u>dead</u>. For in losing one's nefs, one is actually losing one's ego/identity or self-will.

The next part of the equation is sort of mathematical in nature. The use of numbers is <u>not</u> an accurate way to apply it to this example but still it is a great way to introduce the 'death' of the soul concept. So the use of math is only an imaginary way to help in visualizing difficult concepts that can't be seen but can be sensed.

A man is his own little universe or at least that part that makes him a physical, individual entity. Man can hardly even begin to see how he is one with 'nature' and like a universe his body is finely tuned with what is going on around him. He can be balanced within his surroundings or when something is out of kilter, he can be unbalanced and an easy target for disruption known as disease/fever occurs. This does not overcome Divine Destiny but is known by many in the medical profession as good balance within the different created structures (glands, organs and secretions) in the human body. Simply put as many do the saying of having a finely tuned body is appropriate here. The same concept goes for his soul.

Now a man can give, for example, 60% of himself to his Creator Lord while keeping 40% of his own traits (individualism) and this person should be considered as one who is successful in doing a good job. Of course, one should realize once again that this is just an analogy for understanding purposes only and the numbers are not to be taken in any way, shape or form as to being accurate or realistic!

It is reported on the authority of Talha b. 'Ubaidullah that a person with disheveled hair, one of the people of Nejd, came to the Messenger of Allah (may peace be upon him). We heard the humming of his voice, but could not fully discern what he had been saying, till he came nigh to the Messenger of Allah (may peace be upon him). It was then (disclosed to us) that he was asking questions pertaining to Islam. The Messenger of Allah (may peace be upon him) said: Five prayers during the day and the night. (Upon this) he said: Am I obliged to say any other (prayer) besides these? He (the Holy Prophet) said: No, but whatever you observe voluntarily, out of your own free will, and the fasts of Ramadan. The inquirer said: Am I obliged to do anything else besides this?

He (the Holy Prophet) said: No, but whatever you do out of your own free will. And the Messenger of Allah told him about the Zakat (poor-rate). The inquirer said: Am I obliged to pay anything else besides this? He (the Holy Prophet) said: No, but whatever you pay voluntarily out of your own free will. The man turned back and was saying: <u>I would neither make any addition to this, nor will I decrease anything out of it</u>. The Prophet remarked: <u>He is successful</u>, {that is he would enter heaven (Paradise) if he were true to his profession} <u>if he is true to what he affirms</u>. (30) (Sahih Muslim)

This man who wouldn't add anything to his struggles in faith including charity or meditation or indeed any extra effort is still a man of Paradise. He just does the basics (not especially all that easy) but he does them well and he does them with a dogged consistency because he really and truly believes in it. What more can anyone ask?

Imagine, however, a person who spends his life surrendering 90% of himself while keeping only a 10% identity. That person has got to be something special and extremely dedicated to his Creator Lord. Imagine a person achieving a 98% level of surrendering himself to his God. That is just about impossible to conceive of except for the choicest of people. Considering the Grace and Mercy factor from the One God being factored in on each and every stage, one can easily come up with the idea that this person is perfect – for all intent and purposes (31). And considering the New Testament's saying that all have come short of the Glory of God, then that is quite understandable.

That may be very well for the high achievers but it certainly is not going to be adequate for the Messiah. Why? Taking into consideration the alleged statement made by Jesus found in John (10: 30) one can perhaps visualize why (32). He did not claim according to this recorded speech to be <u>almost</u> one with his Creator Lord in intent and purpose (His Will) but that he actually was in oneness in uniformity with His Will. In order to do that he would, hypothetically, have to perform the unheard of task of being 100% perfect.

He will have to give 100% of himself (nefs) and no less than 100% of his soul as a Sacrifice to his Creator Lord. And if he is **allowed** to do this, to accomplish this heretofore unimagined impossible task, then he will be left with exactly 0% of his nefs intact. In other words, there would be nothing left for him to give. Therefore, he would have poured out his soul unto death!

The expression found in Isaiah (pbh) is NOT that his (Jesus') soul gushed out and he died. The expression is that his soul was poured out and when a soul is poured out it is like pouring out liquid from a container. That is, it is poured out in measured quantities under controlled conditions rather than having the container turned immediately upside down creating a total mess in the process.

Can this be proven? According to the records it can be proven but these 'things' seem to be scattered far and wide necessitating a deeper study into things. However, the basics are simple (33). This seems to be quite an extraordinary statement but it is simply true. Basically, it calls mankind to stop and think. It calls on man to follow the rightly guided prophets (in general terms) or that prophet that came to teach or instruct those particular peoples in that age and to follow the pathway laid down for their benefit. After that, it calls on mankind to put their trust in the One who sent these wonderful human beings. In other words, one is called simply to follow the guidance brought (the Sunnah) and to trust in the Wisdom and Planning of the One God.

In Jesus the Christ (pbh) we have an individual who is that new creation – in terms defined by this author – who is shining brightly because he was perfect. Not yet 100% perfect but he was perfect and this is seen from various ways.

His Virgin birth, his NOT being touched by Satan at birth and thus born as what can be said as one definition of being sinless (34). He is like a refined piece of gold being refined for its beauty by having the lesser and baser elements burned away. This is like what happens to refined gold.

One may argue against this but according to the New Testament that holy soul had to do it first for himself for how can he be sinless if he isn't pure himself (35)? So, he must be rendered clean with Allah's Permission. And this he must do for himself first so as not to be a hypocrite but rather to make a real offering as the 'ram' was offered for Abraham's son. This was the offering of his own self (35) to please his Lord in doing His Will (36) to be that special offering (37, 38).

That is still not getting him to the 100% level of that special mark of being the Messiah. For in studying the records as being one, it is noted that there is a mention of his not being touched by Satan at birth like ALL men are even Moses or Muhammad but that he was the one not touched (34).

So the human race under normal conditions does not go forth and break the laws set down for the sons of Adam unless there is a sign of a paradigm shift taking place (38, 39) And part of the notification of that shift taking place and Judgment to come comes from the idea found in scriptures of the likeness of the virgin giving birth in travail. (See appendix A for a fuller explanation. This expression was used before the birth of Jesus or in that period of the expectations of the birth of the Messiah in the Messianic Age).

In order for Jesus (pbh) to become successful (he already is very successful but still the Messiahship is not locked in), he will have to undergo the second refinement making him truly the Messiah (in that exceptional state of sinlessness) to usher in those important periods to come. The first period of course in this understanding is that birth to take place of the man called Muhammad (pbh) because where is the completed building of The Way (40)? The second type of period will be that glorious kingdom promised to the Messiah in leading the blessed souls in that age under The Way as was promised by Him Who keeps His Promise (3, 41).

If this is difficult to conceive, then test the idea!

By having an honest look at Jesus (pbh), one may be forgiven for thinking that he was born with a 'silver spoon' in his mouth. His life and times seem to suggest to the unwary that he must not be human or that he must come from another planet. Take a good close look at his life and one can see that he is only a normal human being that put his <u>total trust in the One God</u> and was rewarded with an excellent station. (42)

He could not get any station by coming in like a thief and stealing it. Therefore, with Allah's Permission and Guidance he had to earn it. Otherwise, his words would ring hallow and his life teachings sound hypocritical in the sense that he is willing to pluck out the mote in other people's eyes but won't look at his own eyes. And this is not what the scriptures were saying (43)!

How is it to a careless person he would look like a man born with a 'silver spoon' in his mouth?

For one thing, he is born of a Virgin. Still following the 'law' for all the sons of Adam must be born of water (the womb) and the spirit. So far he hasn't broken any laws yet. The next thing is that neither he nor his mother is touched by Satan at birth as all men and women must be. So, one must expect that this is a Sign for something especially in the knowledge that this event did <u>not</u> happen after his birth to any other human being (44).

Satan's inability to touch Jesus represents the sinlessness (not meaning the ordinary concept of sin) of being not under the so-called curse of Adam which means being born into the world following that pathway given to <u>all the sons of</u>

<u>Adam</u>. So this is something special. It is special in that a sign is given as to who this person is. That person (as a sign) is simply being not only a high prophet but also the one who has been blessed by his Creator Lord as to the truth in him being the real Messiah and not a fraud.

It is no small feat that a person would be born into the world not being touched by Satan but that is only half the battle. The other half of the battle is more of a titanic struggle in maintaining that purity of birth. For what good would it due the Messiah if he was born this way and then fell flat on his face? No, he must remain in that state of sinlessness (45).

The records do show that he had lots of help in remaining pure. Of course, Jesus (pbh) was not lazy or careless but he must maintain that high level of existence and remain free of sin. That does not mean he was freed from temptations but that he conquered all things that was set before him to conquer.

These things were not according to his plan or doing for like any human being he is not in that position to accomplish these things. Rather, he put his whole trust in Allah and while trusting in Allah's Will, he was allowed to overcome all things and inherit that dominion so rightfully belonging to the true Messiah – a true and dependable slave of Allah.

So being given this special privilege as a birthright, he was surrounded by Angels protecting him from slipping. Not the kind of slipping on a banana peel or twisting his ankle by falling in a hole but in maintaining that perfect perfection of sinlessness (45).

Allah does not require that man give up his nefs for salvation or Paradise would be virtually empty. But in Jesus was shown the Sacrifice of giving up his nefs or surrendering his right of self to be that Sign. So he became that door opener for things to come and he is entitled to be that Messiah.

And how many times did he go forth and prove that he

was the Messiah? His contest with the Satan was won and he took the victory over that bad force. His life was put in danger several times as certain people tried to kill him but all their attempts failed for he had the promise that he would not be disgraced in this world but totally cleared of all falsehood.

And when it came time for him to be taken physically and abused, he maintained his strength like Yusef (pbh) did while he was put in prison. He did not have to defend himself in front of the ignorant hypocrites who had no power over him at all.

And when it came time for those madmen to try and execute him, he being filled with the knowledge and wisdom <u>sent from beforehand</u>, knew that they could not disgrace him but that they who would claim victory by his 'death' would be deluded (46). In truth, he was neither killed nor crucified and he definitely was never put on the cross to be viewed like an animal at a circus.

These struggles for the sake of Allah do not go unrewarded and if man in his faith truly follows the 'way' in love and temperance, then he also becomes blessed (47).

Now people can say that this idea is wrong. But the Sacrifice somewhat discussed in the *Epistle to the Hebrews*, although not a document of purity, shows that Isaiah (pbh) spoke the truth in that Allah was pleased in 'bruising him' and was pleased in His servant's commitment to be that one to prepare the way for the coming of Prophet Muhammad (pbh) (27).

The relationship of Jesus (pbh) to Muhammad (pbh) is not completely understood but that is by no means a requirement in religion. However, we are given some of it and it makes a very logical fit.

Prophet Muhammad (pbh) indeed loves his 'brother' Jesus very much and so should that be because both fit into the category of being excellent prophets and of course they form one brotherhood united in truth (48).

Prophet Muhammad (pbh) as respected as he is in the heavens and the earth is not the only person to have lived on this planet. In fact, before he entered into this life, he did not even know what revelation or faith was. (49).

Yet he was destined to carry the 'banner of praise' for the Creator Lord amongst men. In order to carry that pure Way with the pure Book, his way had to be prepared. In the long view, this preparation began before Adam was alive. For surely Allah is the Best to Plan (23)!

In the short view, this followed on the footsteps of Prophet Jesus (pbh) and another part of the puzzle is put into place. Things like this show a Perfect Plan being unfolded with none able to stop it from happening. Such is the Power of Allah, The Dominate, The Wise!

People may believe that there is only a vague connection between these two men but they would be wrong and this notion comes from several areas including Isaiah (pbh) who describes The Prophet and the Messiah together.

However, with a little balanced and careful thought we might, if Allah Wills, sense why Prophet Muhammad (pbh) loves Jesus very much.

The story the reader is about to receive is a matter of public record. It is not found in some dusty manuscript or incredible source locked away from the public.

Millions of Muslims every day read the Quran. However, before they do, it is a religious practice to be 'clean' before picking up this Book and reading it. One can say that this practice is showing respect for Allah's Revelation to the whole of mankind if they would but accept it.

Now in the annals of revelation to man there has been no book that has been guaranteed to be pure and importantly remain pure – except for one (50, 73)

Well the Old Testament and the New Testament are very good but the paws of villainous individuals have taken their toll in some way, shape or form. And it is not true that a person or organization can't make adjustments to the Quran because they can if they would be that foolish to rush to the Hell-Fire. However, the Quran remains pure and sacrosanct with the guaranteed protection from Allah. Besides this, the original Quran is so overwhelmingly found in numerous places in its original language that a forgery would easily be exposed if there was an attempt to try anything peculiar with the Arabic text.

Reading the Quran and memorizing it is one thing. The actual receiving of That Revelation is another. One would not expect The Prophet (pbh) to be able to receive that Revelation at all. Of course he would be able to receive revelation but That Revelation would seem to be out of the question. Why?

Allah describes His Word, in this case the Quran, in very specific terms (51). So what is wrong in that? Nothing! but Muhammad being like all men was touched by Satan just like Moses, Abraham, Jacob, Noah (peace be upon them all). And with this special Revelation coming for all of mankind and for its use as the bedrock of the 5th Age under the auspicious leadership of the Messiah, it would not take just any mighty man to receive it.

It would take a very special person.

With Allah's description of That Revelation, one might think that Muhammad (pbh) would not be able to bear up under the strain of receiving that most excellent Revelation. Those who think that would probably be right.

Well he did become the chalice for That Revelation and because of this it seems one has reached an impasse on the problem. That is not correct due to the words of Jesus (pbh) found in the Gospel of John (27). According to no less a magnificent personage, Jesus had something to say about it and with a little bit of thought, one can understand something of what is going on.

Quranic Revelation was not easy to receive by the Prophet and sometimes, according to his description, he felt extremely hard pressed at times when he was receiving it (52). However, a close look at the words of Jesus shows a little bit about what has taken place.

In order for the pure to receive the Pure, one would think that one would have to be pure. That is a fact. So how could Prophet Muhammad (pbh) receive That Revelation if he being like us was 'pricked' by the hand of Satan? He couldn't receive it unless that mark all men carried was removed (53).

So as a child in front of witnesses little Muhammad received a very special visitor. That visitor was the high Archangel Gabriel who was ordered by Allah to comedown to Earth and put things according to His Will. And he came and carried with him a special container and a special knife. Then by putting little Muhammad on the ground, he took out his heart and removed that small black speck that all men carry, washed his heart, placed it back and sewed up the opening.

Although it would be more than three decades before the Prophet (pbh) was to receive The Revelation, he had been made ready. The way had been prepared for him so that the world could receive that Good News. Everything Planned and everything in its perfect order and there was no haphazardness about any of it.

The Messiah had to come first so that he could clear the way if one wills for the coming of that mighty Messenger Muhammad (pbh) – the pure leading the way for the pure.

And even other things like the one (Jesus) who has no sin and the other (Muhammad) who had all his sins and future sins forgiven share that trait. So indeed they are close to one another and not just in 'time' (48).

And it shall come to pass that when the Messiah (pbh) dies that death that he as a son of Adam must, he will be buried along side Prophet Muhammad (pbh) and they will rise together as one (4, 5). That is quite an honor in itself – for both of them.

And to understand that there is no other book to be used as that forum for which faith is practiced in the kingdom to come than the Quran and one can sense that indeed the Quran is certainly deserving of being treated with great reverence especially when handled by the hands of men or women.

THE CASE OF WHAT IS SIN

Sin is not so easy to write about because it is a term often abused and not very well understood. However, if an all inclusive definition can be given, some problem found in the book of Isaiah might be made more understandable in the light of sin and the Messiah. Everyone in this world commits sin especially those who write about it because no person is above the law. To be totally sinless as a society would require that particular society to prepare itself for destruction as one famous hadith declares. This hadith states that if a peoples were to remain sinless then Allah would destroy them and bring forth another set of peoples that would sin and go on to seek out His Forgiveness.

That hadith is not asking people to revel in sin but is looking at the practical aspect of one who desires to become better while at the same time appreciating the Creator Lord's Characteristics of His Power, Eminence, Dominion, Love and of course His Grace, Mercy and Forgiveness which are so immense that the mind of man can not properly perceive of His Greatness. We, as fragile souls, are blessed when we can become aware that He is the One and only reason why we exist and to Him all things belong!

According to <u>one definition of sin</u>, sin is the separation from the natural state of being a vicegerent (16). So sin would be the leaving of that state of felicity and holiness from whence one came. Then came the entering into a state of wanderings as was man's destiny from whence he was warned.

So sin is the breaking away to the various degrees of that which separates man from heavenly bliss. But man will, if chosen of God, be purified in this world in the 5th Age of man as promised. So he goes from judgment to Judgment to live without death for ever more.

However, those who remain in sin (estranged from Him by their self will) shall also die and because they will be rejected they also will live. Yet being thrown out of His Mercy by the judgment of their own broken testaments, their life is really death from whence they will be dead. For without Allah's Mercy, a person may live but is considered dead and rejected – but this is for those who will inherit the Hell for ever more.

Now the Messiah became that Sign for the opening for that doorway that was closed. For it doesn't make sense that the 5th Age precedes the 4th Age or that Muhammad (pbh) would be born before Jesus the Messiah (pbh). Things are set in their proper order by a Proper Design because His Plan has been laid out and finely tuned. Therefore, Muhammad (pbh) could not come before Jesus (pbh) but must follow after him in perfect sequence.

Now some say this is foolish gibberish and that one man (by his action grants forgiveness of sins and thus by definition has become a partner to the Living God) so he in effect operates like a god with powers to overlook bad actions of disobedience to the One God.

However, that cannot be because it is **Only** Allah that can forgive sins. So what are sins? Another definition of sins would be that sin is the detraction or separation (loss of that perfection) through which man was created. That is the original state of perfection by which man was originally created. And this example is more understandable, thought provoking and easier to use than the first one given. It is also easier to use in examples.

There are several categories of the forgiveness of sins that can be applied to man. By the end of these examples, it might seem logical that Muhammad (pbh) would be able to forgive sins but that is **Not True**!

The lowest example and indeed an example that is not an excellent one is the example of the patient and the doctor. A man comes in to see a doctor because he had an accident and broke his leg. Now the man's leg was not created or formed broken but was complete and whole. The doctor helps the man and sets his leg in a cast so that it may heal. In effect, the doctor has put the patient on the road to wholeness from whence he had before. Therefore, the doctor had the power granted to him to become a doctor and healed the physical aliment and so he as can be said 'had the power to forgive sins'. Does that mean the patient is guaranteed Paradise and won't go to the Hell-Fire? The answer is NO!

Take the higher example of Jesus (pbh). He healed the sick and even brought the dead to life. His 'wholeness' can be demonstrated from this example found in the New Testament:

And Jesus said, "Somebody has touched me: for I perceive virtue has gone out of me." And when the woman saw that she was not hid, she came trembling, and falling down before him, she declared unto him before all the people for

what cause she had touched him, and how she was healed immediately. Luke (8: 46-47) (54)

His radiant health formed as it were a shield or waves of wellness coming off from his body. So the person that touched him was healed. So, it can be said that Jesus has the power <u>given to him</u> to forgive sins because according to the definition given above, the wholeness was returned to the petitioner. Does this mean that the person healed is guaranteed Paradise and won't go to the Hell-Fire? The answer is NO!

When it comes time to discuss the Prophet (pbh), it is known by those who know that mankind will **swarm** from prophet to prophet and end up going to Muhammad in begging for their own souls due to the torment of unimaginable worry on that special day of disaster whereby the Hell-Fire will look in anticipation for those it will hold. If indeed the real forgiveness of sins is getting away from that awful flesh consuming place of extreme heat and torment, surely the Muslims would attribute the 'power of the forgiveness of sins' to their Prophet. (55, 56, 57)

Indeed Not! How could that <u>falsehood</u> be attributed to him by any responsible and sane believer? It is true that there is a salvation going on but Muhammad (pbh) comes by the **Command** of his Lord and is told what to say by his Lord and therefore he becomes only the object of expression through which certain souls can be saved. (58, 59)

As to Jesus being a representative of mankind (for he is only a man) and being a refined 'new creation' why can't he <u>symbolize that turning point</u> in man's destiny? So that is what he did! For the history of man is <u>filled with such wonders</u> and examples of that symbolization of a dawning of a new era!!! For example, the rainbow appearing after the Great Flood is but a symbol in that era of a turning point.

Are people going to worship the rainbow because of this? That indeed would be a foolish thing to do.

For what <u>one man</u> (Adam) came to <u>symbolize</u> death or the separation of man from that state of harmony (felicity) he was in, <u>another man</u> (Jesus) came to <u>symbolize</u> life or that oneness in intent and purpose with the Creator Lord. And both required the Sacrifice to be given. But the Sacrifice of life is higher than death and so by measured means a soul was chosen to be that offering to Allah – hence, the term Messiah (60).

By no means does this equate with any man being in a state of godhood or having anything to do with being related to God. God Forbid! It was the <u>travail of his soul</u> or the willingness to sacrifice himself as <u>all people</u> of good faith must sacrifice themselves in order to become worthy of putting on that mantel of success.

The travail of his soul first because he must do it for himself in order that he may be worthy of Paradise for just because he lived did not guarantee him success and then for others because a man does not become a Sign only to himself (44).

So why be in dispute concerning this man when the records show that he is **only a man who <u>cannot</u> bear the burdens of another** (61).

FLYING SAUCERS EXPOSED

In this day and age with the vast expansion of knowledge and catastrophes looming on the horizon, mankind is reaching out like never before to the sometime dizzying heights of absurdity. A step back from this often bizarre and loony pace reveals that some people (as if they were being tossed by a violent storm at sea) are searching for solace (any port in a storm) by seeking out various 'gods' to save society from the doom of the terrors of the unknown.

We already have been given that Way and it has a long meaningful history when interpreted and seen correctly; it provides all that mankind needs. However, due to the mystery of the soul and the environs of the Earth on which can be found a complex maze of delusion, it becomes readily apparent that by being an impatient creature (which we are) (62) this system offered up by none other than the One Who Created all things seemingly (as it appears to some) is incomplete and often times is irrelevant.

Talk about being duped! That is being duped. The cases for

this are legion but one of the minor bug-a-boos of modern man's attempt to escape reality comes from the notion of flying saucers and the possible messages that they might have for the lowly human being. It is wise to stop a minute and remember that Abraham, Moses, Jesus and Muhammad were only human beings also.

It goes without saying when all relevant facts are put together that good common sense and an understanding of Islam can handle this flying saucer craze with ease. Even modern science (primitive as it may yet be) is very helpful.

Yes, flying saucers exist but really now! Did one expect them to 'come' to Earth to save mankind? So because they exist, there is no reason to take a button and sew a vest on it especially in the light of the sham that these entities are pulling.

We already have One Savior (the One God) and One Way passed down through the millennia. And it works! There is no need for contemptible upstarts to derail the system unless of course we <u>allow</u> them to do so.

Of course, if one throws away the 'perfect handhold' of the wisdom of true guidance and the Sunnah (the set of guidance and principles) set forth for humanity's protection and growth, and perverts himself willingly he will indeed be at a loss being tossed and turned by the various 'gods' his corruptions created in the first place.

If this sounds like nonsense, it isn't. The road is long and hard but the stakes are high and we were told that long ago so that is that. Besides, being refreshed ever so often by the visitors of great distinction better known as the prophets, we were not left to drift in blind ignorance. But it still doesn't change the fact that the road is long and hard (63).

Now we have run out of being given prophets for the last one finished his job over one thousand four hundred years ago (56). Fortunately, we are not set adrift without the potential refreshing spirit of renewal with the Book and the Sunnah at hand. But the road is long and hard especially amongst diverse cultures, worldly perceptions, gnawing doubts, villainous entities grabbing for our attention, a lethargic state of mind and the lack of good common sense. No wonder that the road is long and hard.

Who can defeat these tyrants especially when the human race has been known to produce its own brand of blood thirsty criminals sent like plagues to torment parts of the human race?

Certainly it is apparent that mankind needs a rest from this merry-go-round circus he has been born into and that is where Faith comes in. But look what happens when one opens the door to that house! Always a few nasty flies are able to get in to spoil the party. Good common sense acts like a flyswatter against these crippling bug-like maggots carrying disease affecting both the mind and the soul.

And these false gods do exist. Like the deranged, constantly changing chameleon-like forces or concepts, they are there to prey on the unwary. For false gods are not only statues but are also other things changing in season with the change of man and his condition. It makes more sense to hammer away at man's weakest point rather than try to assail his strongest one. Hence, inner reflection and contemplation often results in reality coming to the fore while pervasiveness is being beaten back for a while.

And these things are placed in our hands (that is the keys to eternal life) but who is to force one to use them or to even try and understand them? So man has to learn to stand on his own two feet when acknowledging his Sovereign by paying Him true homage and in trusting His Guidance – even though the walls of life are constantly being assailed by a barrage of impotent (forces) devils who gain strength only when fed by the mindless hands of men.

Once again we go back to the lack of common sense providing food for these dark forces to act upon. What does one expect when a hungry tiger knocks at the door to gain entry? Shall we let him in? If so, then we must be prepared to take the consequences.

A looming crisis of near epidemic proportions has been unfolding. This epidemic has affected nearly one billion people around the world due to certain news events especially from 'western' countries. It concerns the subject of 'flying saucers' from outer space.

In my first book, *The Shining Light of Islam*, I dealt very briefly on this topic. However, newer information has come forward which has tended to vindicate what was written and the beautiful thing about it is that these things can be documented successfully and followed logically with good common sense.

With the help of logic, psychology, science and religion, mankind is in the position of pinning down the flying saucer phenomenon with complete surety. One reason why that might not happen so easily is that people might want their own fantasies kept alive even in the face of documented, hard evidence.

A library could be filled with books and articles written about this flying saucer phenomenon as well as some of man's visions about what 'they' may mean to the human race. One thing is for certain. It is incredible how the mind of man works in all of its varied activities.

A world that has seen such stalwarts as Abraham, Moses, Jesus and Muhammad should acknowledge that that is enough for man to dwell on but apparently some things become lost from the mind necessitating great flights of fantasy.

Some current thoughts put forward by the so called 'believers' of aliens from outer space are that these creatures are here to protect man against self destruction, to guide man into the future, to someday announce that they are our gods who have created us or aided in our development from the monkey or to just plain observe mankind as he develops – sort of like space sociology 101.

The biggest problem faced by believers and skeptics alike was in trying to fit the various pieces together about this phenomenon to form a logical whole. Now it can be done and documented although there will still be plenty of people who will prefer the far out explanations rather than the truthful one. Hence, societies like the Flat Earth Society still survive.

So the misconceptions about 'flying saucers' is legendary. If these things exist, and they do, what could they be? What logically could they be based on the latest modern research that is easily documented?

Over one thousand four hundred years ago Prophet Muhammad (pbh) did discuss the issues but it takes a measure of thought to put it into a proper perspective. In other words, it was not his job to come and instruct man about flying saucers 101 but rather to discuss about Truth and Salvation. Islam has more depth to it than just rituals – though of a highly important nature – and who knows of this are they who dwell upon Islam in its beauty and depth.

The case for flying saucers in brief

Through the late 1940s, 50s and the early 60s the flying saucer bug caused a lot of confusion especially to the military-intelligent agencies handling it. The issue wouldn't go away even under pressure of stigmatizing it in the publics' eye. However, as has been shown in the past the military-intelligent complex sometimes performs as if they have two left feet, but that isn't always the case.

Being completely buffaloed by this tantalizing phenomenon, the government had no choice but to turn to certain scientists who were given certain classified information and asked an important question. The question was, "**If** these things (flying saucers) exist and there is no real proof that they do, what probable power source could they be using to propel themselves?"

That question and the scientists' answer would go on to form the whole key to the (reality) of the flying saucer issue and would lead to some strange undertakings by the military-intelligence complex.

After some reflection on this issue, the scientists concerned gave the answer. The answer was that this phenomenon (if it truly existed at all) would, according to the evidence presented to them, probably use some form of electro-magnetic energy for propulsion.

End of story? No, it is not over by a long shot. The military-intelligent machine assigned to this undertaking may not be bright lights but they aren't completely out of touch with reality. They knew of some of the quality reports, films, etc that they had but couldn't make heads or tails out of them. They also had several good files of radar reports. The problem with radar is that it at times acts twitchy and therefore is not completely 100% reliable. However, if and only if two things can successfully correlate the existence of this phenomenon, then no matter what they are, they in fact are real and of course exist.

So what was missing was the 'fingerprint' to nail down the issue. That may not sound fantastic but it was about to become fantastic. Wondering what these things were and where they could possibly be coming from could take 10 million years to figure out and that is fruitless. However, it is so typical of the military-intelligent complex to think of the physical issue. If a 'fingerprint' could be lifted, it would mean two important things. First, they exist. Finally, and this will go on to explain a few things, if it exists, then it can be built!

That is, it can eventually be manufactured by the secret agency given charge over the project. But first, the fingerprint had to be found. It was found. That is, a correlation between radar reports and an electro-magnetic signature given off at the same time and place showed that these objects were real. Whether an object is made of cheese or metal doesn't mater. Its existence can now be verified.

The following information to be presented was taken from the *Discovery Science* channel and these programs can be checked and researched for their accuracy. The deductions, however, are up to the individual.

In the 60s, or 70s there appeared in Canada some interesting towers constructed for some unknown purpose. They didn't have anything to do with weather measurements or tracking guided missiles. In fact, they seemed to be totally useless. The only thing that these towers were good for was to measure electro-magnetic energy from anything that would be flying overhead. Birds, planes, rockets or kites would be left out in the cold so basically it would measure totally nothing and be rendered totally useless – an example of someone spending money on absolutely nothing and for no purpose. And since it was a shot in the dark and not the publics' business anyway, who would be in the know to ask the right questions?

Well, they did get to measure some 'hits' and one hit was sent down to America labeled and underlined as being from a UFO. Why send the report to America and why label it as a UFO? It doesn't take a genius to figure that one out.

If radar also got a hit and tracked this unknown thing in the same area, then radar (in this case) can't be accused of acting up and providing false blips due to temperature inversions. Therefore, only one possible conclusion can be drawn from this experiment. Something that is using electro-magnetic energy for propulsion has just been fingerprinted. And if it can be fingerprinted, it is not a fairytale but actually exists. And if it exists, it can be built.

The *Discovery Science* channel showed in another program an elderly man explaining how to build a <u>primitive</u> flying saucer. Not only did he talk about it (saying a high school student could do it) he actually <u>demonstrated</u> how to do it! He took a circular object and with an electromagnet placed inside, ran a large current of electricity into it. The object rose in the air, hovered and then the wires from the attached cable started to burn up.

If a high school kid could do it, imagine what some high powered scientists could do under secret funding. But don't get too excited because of the following:

Take a modern car and go into an imaginary time machine back several hundred years into the thick of the Industrial Revolution. Show the real car to the scientific minds back then and tell them to build one. Then take the car back to one's normal time. How well do you think those scientists of yesteryear would do in accomplishing the deed? Not very well at all!

This answers the question about that infamous place found in America called, Area 51. Of course this area is mostly about research into futuristic weapons giving the military the edge on the enemy but other things go on in that place which is said to be guarded more heavily than Fort Knox.

To build such an object to travel across the United States would require a 3,000 mile long lead cord. That idea being rejected, one finds the next step more logical by placing the power source inside the object rather than outside. Of course the two biggest problems remaining that still have to be solved would be to keep people who would travel inside alive for more than a few seconds because of the type of power source used and how to control the object without it blowing up or crashing instantly.

Would years of research be needed to accomplish this seeing that scientists would be literally working in the dark on this matter? No, decades and lots of them would be needed to iron out these problems.

In the same program (?) came another breakthrough. A man who was bothered by certain 'visitations' but who now works for a hospital was explaining the complexities of those who have claimed to have been taken aboard a flying saucer (a case for alien abductions). The bottom line was that <u>no such thing exists</u> as those people related it as a reality but <u>another</u> kind of reality was occurring which could be explained and measured somewhat.

It seems that a certain part of the brain can be somehow manipulated (by what?) into making an unreal experience seem completely real rather than imaginary. This manipulation can be investigated, mapped and measured to a certain degree and that part of the brain has been located and that special area inside that part has been more or less pinpointed. All of this has been documented and while further research is continuing, some scientists can and have induced certain believable but totally unreal conditions on subjects who have volunteered for these tests.

What does this have to do with Islam? Think of about a billion people being 'infected' to various degrees by this phenomenon which some would call a disease of sorts. If a person carrying lots of food walks by a hungry man and says, "You are not of my skin color, nationality or faith, so why should I care about your condition?" that would seem to be atrocious.

So what is this phenomenon all about? According to the knowledge found in Islam, there is a race of beings different from human beings in that they were created from smokeless fire. They are called Jinn and amongst these Jinn are the good and bad Jinn. Moreover, like mankind (from highly evolved societies to present but rare still existent Stone Age peoples) they exist in different categories with presumably different formats. There are Jinn that live under the earth, on the earth, even inside the human being (giving urges) and those who live mainly in the sky – and all have their various but different functions.

Even though Jinn don't have our skin color and don't wear American flags in their lapels, they have a right to exist and they perform a purpose – for good or for evil or anything in between. Man might suggest that this planet belongs to him alone. Perhaps that is what Adolph Hitler thought also. The important thing is not to lose one's head over the issue.

Prophet Muhammad (pbh) described how a certain type of Jinn courses through the veins of man like the blood. The human brain and that center of the brain associated with the 'abduction' scenario of course must receive a flow of blood. It is obvious what is taking place in these so-called abduction scenarios but the specific reasons, except for causing disruptions on the human subject, are not.

As for flying saucers sometimes exploding in the air well that happens also. Pieces have been found and taken in for analysis. Taking out the mostly fraudulent cases, the so-called strange materials were analyzed as being made of regular earthly material. Other evidence such as photographs or films has also been taken.

Several photographs taken from a naval ship later dubbed as 'The Trinidade Island Photographs' and reportedly seen by over 50 witnesses show a flying saucer object changing shape while engaged in flying. If these photographs are real, then imagine a 'machine' being constructed during flight! Most of the best pictures produced for examination have been grainy and show blobs of light like the famous 'Lubbock lights' film.

However, there are cases when a solid type object has been photographed showing a distinct shape but these are not every day occurrences.

Common sense can lead one to certain conclusions based on logical intelligence and away from fanciful thinking. It is not the primary purpose of man's sojourn on Earth to become involved with this life-form especially since some of them are not well-wishers of mankind as in being devilish in nature. However, everything has its limitations or areas that cannot or will not be tolerated if stepped across and that is enough for man to utter his praise for his Creator Lord's Protection.

The use of common sense when dealing with this strange phenomenon is especially helpful. One must take a look at common logic and ask some very important questions.

If another civilization from outer space would be visiting the Earth, what precisely would be the best logical approach for them to use?

Taking into consideration the knowledge that we have been given concerning the Creator Lord and His Awareness and Dominance, the universe with its vast size but limited physics, one would think the so-called space aliens would be able to find the most logical point of contact. That logical point of contact that would provide the greatest exchange of information with the least interference would be the organization called SETI.

Contacting SETI after observing Earth would be the most logical thing to do. Finding out how to reach out to this organization would be quite simple for anyone with an average intelligence. Just looking at their equipment dotted all over the place would not be hard to find. And contact with that organization by using the same simple means that SETI uses to listen in space for 'intelligent' signals does not require a genius type of mentality – especially if the humans have been doing it for decades.

Why would one want to use SETI? It would provide the safest link in understanding various men and the Earth's culture and history in a non-threatening environment plus having the advantage of getting away from homespun and often fatally flawed philosophies and half truths and other con jobs put forth by political agencies looking out for their own advantages.

But that has not happened. Instead one finds bizarre stories featuring 'aliens' who seemingly run around the universe at will and doing strange things that would be considered in most earthly cultures having 'Divinely' sent records for the uplifting of man as bordering on sin and arrogance and just plain foolishness.

But can we expect 'aliens' who don't look like us or feel as we feel to operate using 'human' logic? There is a difference between 'human logic' and what can be called the Universal Logic. By reading the Quran, as strange as that may seem to some people, one can get a sense of the <u>Universal Logic</u> as it would apply to all of the creation (seen or unseen, known or unknown) and what happens when this logic goes out the proverbial window. So essentially one can take the story of gravity, for example, and know that under every condition gravity will operate in some predetermined way based on certain laws that interact with this force. Otherwise, if gravity had a mind of its own and no responsibility to perform according to its set boundaries, then one could consider gravity as either a false god or a renegade force deciding what and when and under what conditions to operate.

Islam provides a background for this phenomenon but does not go to great lengths to enter into that which goes off the beaten path of man's existence or that which is essentially none of man's concern or to put it bluntly his business. The message is to concentrate on the job at hand and don't worry about the 'fringe element' or that what is not needed for Salvation. So in other words, concentrate on the job at hand and leave alone that what does not concern one. That does <u>not</u> mean to go around without thinking or to become mindless robots. For example, we do know that the Sun exists and that while on Earth we need that life-force that it is giving off. Furthermore, some have used the knowledge of the Sun's happenings to improve their farming techniques. However, should life stop because we must find the exact date of the Sun's extinction? The answer is no because that is not in our hands and that has nothing to do with us but if some want to investigate the probable causes and learn something of what is perceived as the physical laws of the universe, then that is all right also.

Prophet Muhammad (pbh) gave specific instructions on how to chase these pestering and meddling tricksters away if they interfere with the human being. Otherwise, leave them alone and generally speaking they will leave you alone.

It is interesting that the flying saucer phenomenon has affected a lot of people <u>with a lot of paranormal events</u> being thrown in the process causing a general waste of time and mind-set. After all, who needs Moses, Jesus and especially Muhammad when at any moment we are about to be saved by little gray/green men from planet Zorn.

What helps to keep this flying saucer fantasy alive are basically two things: titillation and money. Titillation happens because some people desire 'tales of the ancients' to fantasize about. Money is partly to blame because a lot of writers make a living off of feeding this titillation. That is quite a maddening cycle.

If anyone is interested in reality and wants more information about this subject, it is advisable to go only to the proper sources acceptable from an orthodox Islamic point of view. Otherwise, one can just keep on chasing after the 'pot of gold' found at the end of the rainbow.

THE WALL

In two of my previous books, *The Real Holy Grail: The Messiah on Trial* and *He Is Not My Ancestor*, a few tidbits were passed on concerning ages gone by. Perhaps it made some humorous break for any scientist that may have pondered over it. After all, it is really out of the normal type of theory pushed forward by many of the scientific community that we have become accustomed to.

It would also cause a tremendous amount of havoc with today's formulated pet theories and put many a scientific mind behind the proverbial eight ball. Why? Well for one thing, the world would be turned upside down as far as history is concerned and a lot of self-indulgent delusions would be punctured.

In other words, mankind would get not only a swift kick in the pants (often where is intellect seemingly lies) but also a swift dose of reality as to where he might lie. Reforming history is no mean feat but the ego deflation seemingly is worse. Not only that, but throw Islam into the mix and we have an interesting situation brewing up which most scientists would love to dodge.

Science is a lot better than witchcraft but it isn't the end all or the great liberator of humanity either. And to wean ourselves off the notion that space, time and further research will turn us into 'gods' is yet another bitter pill to swallow.

Instead of trying to conquer space and trying to find out if Mars once had a microbe living on it, the knowledge of something of our past might help us more to guide us to our future. How? By facing the realities of life better is how. Of course science has come a long way in trying to break down barriers of ignorance as well as to establish new and wonderful opportunities for mankind and that is something to be thankful for. However, some hold to the position that the more relief we get due to advancement in cerebral thinking, the worse off we have become. That is not the fault of science but rather lies squarely on the shoulders of this planet's inhabitants.

They say the drive for knowledge is inherent in man's soul or mind. Would it be more fruitful to spend hundreds of billions of dollars on helping man advance in dignity rather than searching for possible microbes (dead or alive) that perhaps are as intelligent as some men who lack wisdom but in reality cannot think or communicate with man?

In other words, space exploration is not a high level, medium level or low level priority but one that is a bottom of the barrel priority.

Upon saying this, it probably won't be taken kindly about the discussion of 'The Wall'. The Wall exists and although its roots have not been photographed as of yet, its later stages have been. The extension or outer boundaries have been photographed numerous times near what is called the Bimini Road in about 6 meters of water (Bimini is a district of the Bahamas). This of course is not The Wall but a beginning leading to The Wall and of a much later date. Nevertheless, The Wall does exist and is close by this photographed site.

One way to dodge this issue is to proclaim that the sea built that extension and therefore it is a natural formation. This leads one to proclaim that it therefore is not a big deal. The case is solved and it is time to move on to more realistic things.

Well, before one jumps to any unwarranted conclusions, let us go back before The Wall existed and work with some type of individual who is more accustomed to be less excitable than the average scientist – the geologist.

Now it was admittedly stated in one of my books that Noah (pbh) the first prophet of what we would recognize as such lived over 30,000 years ago. Geologists are not in a position to talk about this sincere man because they don't deal with such things. However, they do deal with rock strata and can give fair to good estimates when huge and devastating floods spread across part of the Earth. It is this information found in the various strata of rock that dates certain events in history.

By following (testing) the territory affected by the 'Great Flood' it would be quite a coincidence to find out that over 30,000 years ago a Great Flood occurred in the areas as stated in the Holy Records. This of course depends upon finding those supposed coordinates where the 'mother of all floods' took place.

It is true that this will not prove Noah (pbh) existed but it is one whale of a coincidence that is hard to ignore.

So what about The Wall? It can either be found to have been built by the sea as a natural formation made of what is called beach rock or if not, then it was built by men for the purpose of being part of a great seaport for world-wide trade some 18,000 years ago. This sounds utterly fantastic to the average citizen but to most scientists it would sound absurd if not psychotic based on the current history of <u>what we know</u> as the development of human civilization. Also, people might like to know how we got from A to M without going through the rest of the letters.

To solve this puzzle go to the geologist.

Now it is true that the sea can make a lot of things but I wouldn't go so far as claiming the sea made a giant seaport. Moreover, I don't claim that the atmosphere built the Empire State building either even though the atmosphere is quite uplifting and beneficial.

The geologist already knows that if The Wall exists and is a manmade structure (there are not too many choices in this matter) it was built more than three years ago. It had to have been built when that surface now underneath the photographed roadway by quite a few meters was at one time very close to the surface. Furthermore, being an alleged seaport makes a lot of sense and being a huge seaport would not make any sense at all if only small rowboats moved only a few meters back and forth for fear of falling off the edge of the world. Huge seaports are built for world-wide trade and not for fun and games.

Seaports mean trade with various civilizations and in this case trade on a monumental scale by the looks of it. If that is so, then a computer (not desktop) like an advanced astrolabe had better be used for navigation purposes. These ideas and those that can be spun off that type of society require that particular society be well-versed in the sciences. In other words, the builders of The Wall could only come from a highly advanced culture.

According to the above logic any engineers who might be privileged to study this structure would concur that a very advanced form of society would be needed to plan, construct, build and maintain that edifice.

All of this may sound fine but the <u>current</u> viewpoint as to man's abilities 18,000 years ago puts man in the just forming post Alley Oop era of cartoon fame. In other words, men had the ability to paint cave walls and wear clothing and of course procreate but that would hardly grant man a license for superior advancement. Therefore, 12,000 to 10,000 years ago man just started to get into the hang of farming and could hardly be expected to count higher than 100. 18,000 years ago the Neanderthal man was already extinct by only a few thousand years paving the way for modern man to crawl out of the cave and into prominence.

The Wall would tear that philosophical mumbo-jumbo down and would make out such worthy notables as Columbus and Magellan not fit to be lowly cabin boys for that so-called advanced society. All of that seems problematical to the point of ridiculousness except for one minor element – man's insatiable curiosity.

If a ship loaded with golden doubloons was spotted in the depth of water The Wall presumably exists at, treasure hunters would flock to the area and being equipped with modern technology literally suck up the sand to uncover the loot. The technology is there anyway even though it is labor intensive. And to think that things have been recovered from the Titanic, which was a far more difficult operation, gives one a chance to think.

In addition to this, modern day treasure hunters don't have to be reminded that seaports are a peculiar place. Things always seem to get dropped overboard by various means and that would translate into much needed artifacts worth lots of money. And if there is a real breakthrough find which seems almost certain, then these artifacts would be considered priceless in another way since they would be considered a staggering find of importance from deep into antiquity.

Up until now The Wall remains a mystery generally put in the realm of something built and laid down by the sea – a sea that should be recruited to help people in areas where there appears a housing shortage. Or it can be taken as just an object that is just there but whatever it is, it too has a destiny that is waiting to be unfolded – a destiny that should bring the world into a better focus about the wonders of its past and man's relationship to the One God.

STORIES

There were three men who met by the seashore of a vast immeasurable ocean. Looking out upon this unending and vast expanse of water with its splendid waves and sensing its depth to be impenetrably deep, the men stood by the seashore as indistinguishable specks of dust that would draw no notice from a passerby.

Each man held a part of that infinite body of water in their hand. The first man held a teacup filled with that precious water. The second man held an eyedropper filled with that water while the third man could only capture but a molecule of its essence.

All three men looked at each other and began to laugh. It was not a boisterous laughter but laughter in the form of praise for the One Who made all things.

The first man, who had the teacup turned to his companions and said, "What we have been given is precious beyond thought but compared to this immeasurable depth of an infinite ocean, it is as if we are holding nothing at all."

There once was a man called ibn Taymiyah. In a way he was like a farmer who planted some seeds. And some of these seeds grew into marvelous trees that were laden with heavy, sweet tasting fruit. And some of these seeds grew into spindly trees that bore rotten fruit. While the goodly fruit from the goodly trees were harvested for a holy banquet, the foul tasting fruit from the sickly trees were hewn down and thrown into the fire.

Centuries later, a few people sat around wondering just what kind of farmer that man ibn Taymiyah was. However, one man that sat amongst the group said, "It is not an appropriate question to ask what kind of farmer he was. For a farmer doesn't broadcast seeds in a vacuum. He broadcasts them on soil. Therefore, the real question is what kind of soil are we? For goodly soil raises goodly fruits and bad soil raises bad fruits." One gentleman amongst the group asked, "What do you mean by that?" The first man replied, "Don't blame the farmer; blame the soil."

Once upon a time there was a strange man passing through a very small and insignificant village. As he was passing by, he saw a sad, little man sitting by himself with a disconsolate look on his face. The wanderer said to the little, sad man, "What is troubling you my friend?" The sad man said, "I cannot read or write. In fact, I cannot do any particular job well. You see, without education I seem to have been left well behind. I cannot even repair cars or work on a computer that I have heard so much about. All I'm known for is the one who has memorized the Quran and I'm known to recite it with a fair voice."

"So what is wrong with that," said the stranger? "But you see," said the sad man all the while keeping his head bowed down to the ground, "I cannot tell about even what I recite for I don't even know the language or the meaning of what I say." The stranger said, "Don't you trust in your Creator Lord?" "Yes I do," said the sad man.

"Good," said the stranger, "But why do you want to exchange a crown of gold for a crown of tin? Don't you know that for every letter you recite out of every word amplifies your reward? The world passes judgment on its own and the world will vanish. Your Lord passes Judgment and it shall not vanish but will endure. So put your trust in Him Whose Trustworthiness cannot be disputed."

The little, sad man became happy once again for now he had a purpose and a handhold that never breaks. He was about to thank the stranger but when he looked up to give his thanks, the stranger was not found and none can remember even seeing that strange man who visited this certain small out of the way village. But the little man knows and he is not sad anymore.

I once went to a hotel where a convention was taking place. Inside this hotel I was told that they had a room reserved for contemplation. Inside that room was a table with a sign saying, 'saying of the day (57), please contemplate about it in silence for one hour'.

I noticed a dark haired man who looked rather handsome and athletic going inside. After one hour he came out looking ashen-faced and kind of wobbly on his feet all the while mumbling something inaudible. Even his darkened hair seemed changed as its luster turned somewhat grayish. On his unsteady way out of the hotel, he dropped his name tag which I picked up and returned to the main desk. The desk clerk read the name on it and put it in the slot where it belonged so that it could be picked up later.

The next day I saw another good-looking gentleman

walk into that room. He stayed one hour but he came out of that room in a somewhat different way than the first gentleman. He didn't look happy. In fact, he looked awfully bored while mumbling something about 'a waste of time'. He also dropped his name tag as he was probably in a hurry to get to some important place. I picked up his name tag and handed it to the desk clerk like I did the first one. The desk clerk looked puzzled for a moment because the name tag had simply no name on it.

Well, as I had an engagement outside the hotel, I left the lobby and proceeded out the door. As I was leaving the hotel, I turned back and saw the desk clerk fiddle with the nameless tag and then while shrugging his shoulders; he threw it into the garbage.

There were once two outstanding architects of well-known fame who worked for a company called Concepts and Constructs. Both of these men could theoretically design a house that would be admired by one and all for its extreme function-ability, beauty, sturdiness and practicality. Both men could do it but only one of them did it.

One day a rare and most terrible storm suddenly hit the area where these two men worked. This rather freakish storm was extremely violent and destructive. The residents of that once small and sleepy city rushed to enter the shelters of their houses for protection.

The architect who got around to actually building his house survived the worst storm in recorded history bruised and battered but still alive. The other architect joined the ranks of those who were lost – never to be found again.

CONCEPTS AND CONSTRUCTS

Happy is the man who can practice faith in simplicity while building up his character in doing deeds for the sake of Allah alone.

For the rest of us, being in the world is like being put through a meat grinder or even caught standing in the middle of a freeway with lots of fast moving traffic whizzing by. People have to learn how to slow down and take life in small doses.

This world is filled with more traps than a legion of furriers might have (63). It's a small wonder that a lot of people, and I do mean a lot of people, view religion as a topic to be avoided like the plague.

To understand religion is to understand people and to understand people is to understand religion for religion is oftentimes the outer covering that people wear. Life is full of unreality and contradictions and worldly plots and plans that are so dodgy that it is a wonder that people survive at all.

Basically since we all are filled with 'the spirit' one can see great divergence in this world. But stop and think a bit! There are only two categories that reckless men fit into when poisoning the soul (69). Of course these categories have multiple sub-categories but still there are only two broad sweeping categories no matter what delusions a person has about himself.

One is that a person says, "I believe" but the person really deep down doesn't really believe because his heart won't let him believe in the reality of <u>accountability</u> in some form or fashion. To that person even if his mind registers the words, the idea just doesn't appear to ring true in his heart.

The second thing is that man is filled-up with himself so much that his delusions become his pathway for success. One can worship a statue or a philosophy and that is his goal to reach out and make it happen. That is his way which assails or sub-plants His Way – in his dreams!

It sounds moronic but it is simply true. False gods can be anything a person puts together that defies the Truth. Fortunately, some people have been known to wake up to that 'clarion call' of Real Reality before they die.

Who is in charge? I don't care how many titles a man has next to his name (55), if that person is truthful, he will simply give and show the truth (70). And that ends that story!

There are lots of reasons why people called Christians have become somewhat befuddled by the stain of philosophical nonsense put upon a once most acceptable belief system. My other books talk about some of these reasons. However, written inside the New Testament the words of Jesus (pbh) cuts to the quick (68).

It not only cuts to the quick, it refers back to the saying number (71). Of course one cannot read another person's heart to see if he is an unclean, trickster of a dog or swine ready, willing and able to transform beautiful and dynamic concepts into plain, unadulterated trash.

And those meddling, phony philosophers could turn on the 'body of the faithful' once they were handed the truth and then went forth to pollute and create a nightmarish made-up religious philosophy which would literally cause real religion to be torn apart. It was not only the religion being torn apart but history is filled with such physical violence against other human beings that sickens the hearts of men. Hence, the term 'rend' is used.

People have a mind of their own so let them choose and hopefully they will choose wisely and that is as far as it goes because no one can be forced to go against his own soul's desire and be of those who are of the sincere.

So the best concepts and constructs to utilize is **not** philosophy but real character building following the Sunnah (ways and practices given) with a humble heart. That is a known product that gives real and tangible results not fluff and self-delusions.

People are asked to seek out knowledge and the best of knowledge is that which enforces the concept of Divine Unity on which **all things are based**. The further one gets away from Divine Unity, the further one gets mired in what is called 'sin'. Although most men do not comprehend this because the thoughts on the importance of Divine Unity are varied, the importance of Divine Unity just so happens to be the Primary Directive in Islam or that which is called the first Pillar in Islam.

So that is the key element or secret in religion. The Divine Unity concept upon which all things must be judged and it goes back to the saying number (69) as well as what is found in the Quran as to why Allah created men and Jinn. It was but to worship Him and Him alone.

Allah is He Who has given Himself Names and those who claim to believe in Divine Unity do lie when they try to cancel out any one of His Names. Those who claim that the One God is for them alone or favors them above others because of just belonging to a certain race or creed are trying to void the Name – THE TRUTH. And those who declare that the One God has a son or an offspring are trying to void the Names – THE ONE, THE UNIQUE. So, not all who claim that they believe in Divine Unity are telling the truth.

When all is said and done, the Majestic Might and Majesty of the Supreme Creator Lord causes men, who take the time to contemplate, to be filled with awe and wonder. It is no wonder that if all the innumerable Angels, Jinn, mankind and other creatures we know nothing about would come together with His Permission to form and plan what He Formed and Planned, then their combined efforts would end up in chaos. So, it is no wonder that those who take the time to contemplate about His Excellence have found no words worthy enough to praise Him as He should be praised.

We can only follow gifted men. Men like us (prophets), but more gifted and inspired in their teachings of praise for the One Who has no partners or peers. And these prophets humbled themselves in the dust in awe of Him Who has no needs nor suffers from any lack. So, if the foolish want to compare themselves with something, let them compare themselves to the prophets and then learn wisdom. And that wisdom would be that we all fall far immeasurably short of those valiant men.

Then comes the tears of wisdom to show gratitude to The One Who gave us life and Who will cause us to die and will cause us to be raised up. He will show us the records of that what we did and He is the One Who will recreate us again. It is to Him and His Messenger that the successful owe their allegiance. That is wisdom and that is salvation!

CONCLUSION

The whole effort behind my seven books can be simply boiled down into one thought. That thought is that there has always been and always will be but One God and that there was given to mankind from amongst themselves a One brotherhood of prophets forming a harmonious unity of truth. That there is only One Messiah that shall lead the righteous on his return and that there is only One Way shown by that dynamic but of course completely human messenger known as Muhammad (pbh). Other than that, what is there?

O there are lots of secondary and tertiary things which make life interesting but hair splitting is not one of them. Part of the destiny of man is to figure things out and move along the road that gives success – not as some would define success but as He (the One God) defined it and sent it down unto mankind.

Is there anyone who can gain 100% Perfection of and by himself? The answer is of course **NO**. It has to be granted either in this world or in the Hereafter but by His Grace, Mercy and Forgiveness.

Once again the 'conjectures' put forward concerning such topics as flying saucers, The Wall, the Six Ages of man theory and the era of Noah might bring heaps of derision from some circles. So what? Find solace in the old adage of "he who laughs last; laughs best." One can say that these things at least breakup the monotony of a hum-drum existence.

And why not turn to Islam? Who are the people making it a criminal offense? Obviously, a thoughtless, shallow individual has no love or respect for his Creator Lord and is heedless of the Hereafter.

Well the contest of 'Trust' didn't turn out to be a cakewalk so what else is new? Life is life after all and hopefully the individual will seek to put it to good use.

APPENDIX A

The Epistle To The Hebrews

At one time this document existed in its original form but it does not have that distinction anymore. The *Epistle to the Hebrews* is a quasi-gnostic document found in the New Testament containing some good gems of information about the Messiah-soul. However, it is too obvious that this document has gone under the knife and manipulated to a certain degree.

This document in original form could only have been written a decade or so after Paul's death to another kindred spiritual sect. It seems Rome had not yet received the prominent stature as the center of learning which it would receive many decades later.

This document is for instruction and reminder which would operate in combating creeping theological errors already rife within the community.

The author of this document was a well-known and respected person and that is one reason why the 'handed down' and reworked document does not now bear his name. In other words, his name was purged from the document for in later years it would be difficult to go back and find the real sentiments behind this document.

Several things point in that direction. First, the first couple of chapters have been cleverly altered just a bit so as to give a certain point of view emerging at the time. Second, the crass outright forgery of just what son of Abraham (pbh) was offered in sacrifice can help date this retouched document to the early part of the second century.

The Old Testament version which stumbles on this issue is unclear as to who the real first son of Abraham was but hastens to declare the son to be Isaac (pbh) and this was done for obvious reasons. But Jesus (pbh) declared that to another set of peoples the mantel of authority would pass (64).

A close inspection of the records shows that the person who was responsible for the forgery just doesn't get it at all. Jesus, his companions and the next two generations were Jews (under the line of Isaac) being reformed Jews under the new law (65). There are two definitions of this 'new law'. One definition concerns a relaxing of the law for the benefit of the people under new Judaism. The other meaning is that a Paradigm Shift has taken place for that which will come (The Great News) in the form of that completed Way in the future (39, 41). And even the gentile converts were under the new law being instructed in the Sunnah of Jesus until the various sects wrangled with each other – each having a part of the truth which they overemphasized in competition with other groups.

Therefore, the person who forged this document made the big mistake of emphasizing the line of Isaac which by its own definition must soon come to an end of dominion with the resurrection of Jesus. Later a new prophet, but of the other Semitic line, would be raised up and he would be referred to as 'That Prophet'. (See appendix B for a discussion about this).

Finally, the mentioning of Timothy and the 'Italians' was thrown into the document to give it the touch of antiquity and the proof of authenticity so that it could be passed off as a document worthy of all credibility.

The *Epistle to the Hebrews* does contain a lot of good, solid information about that stalwart soul known as Jesus the Christ (pbh). However, it is a document mostly beneficial for scholars and deep thinkers and doesn't offer much real meat on character building. So in retrospect it doesn't perform much of a function unless one is in a position to pause and reflect on the vicegerency of Jesus and his representation as undergoing the struggles to be that special Sign unto mankind as a complete human being.

It is also a document that can be used to argue for or against the physical crucifixion. That may sound odd but that may explain why this document has actually survived the ravages of time. It is obvious that the 'physical crucifixion' is totally ignored but it is also obvious that others could use this document to try and prove the so-called crucifixion of Jesus. So this gives us a lesson right quick.

One cannot expect from gnostic writings (even if they are true) to be understood at the drop of a hat. But if they are true, they have to pass a test and that test must be that there shall be in no way a disagreement amongst the scriptures. So the idea is set that Jesus the son of Mary (pbh) is a Sign unto man. And as a Sign he becomes a part of Allah's Plan for those who understand. But one should not be dazzled by the Sign but only by the Sign Maker – the One and Only God!

It is infinitely better to place one's foot on a more stable and solid ground. So, how can man do that? Well, that is quite simple. The best 'document' of all to read is The Quran. So now you know.

The Dead Sea Scrolls point out that long before the birth of Jesus the son of Mary – the eagerly sought righteous one to be born was the mysterious concept of the virgin woman giving birth in the desert 'in travail'. And that the successful part of the human race and also like him who was to come was likened to a 'woman in travail' because the gates of Paradise could not be opened by mere chance.

In other words the expectation of this event like the expectation of the mother with child was heightened as for the looking forward to the promise that would come (in this case a holy child to be born and the much sought after event of the next prophet).

The heightened expectation can be understood from the following. Were we to spend an endless eternity of striving for faith for nothing? Would countless eons pass and still the Promise go unfulfilled? The promise that a pure child would grow protected by his Lord (45) unto fulfillment of conquering sin and thereby opening the way for That Prophet to enter into the world completing that Faith by laying the foundations of the Way so that Way would be established as The Way and be That Way to be taken up by him who by His Lord's Desire would lead that kingdom of paradise on Earth on his second coming.

So born into the world came him who was called The Righteous Servant of Allah that through his Sacrifice of offering himself up to sinlessness and being cleaned to perfection of giving up his soul in completeness such that he had nothing more to offer – being that which holds all of us back – he then gave of himself so that the new law would be put into effect (39).

First for himself, for how can the guilty lead those who are to be purified? Then, for that creation called the sons of Adam to receive that 'new-testament' called in Arabic, Islam (66, 67).

Men who are hasty say that this is wrong because they want their way to be that way but their way is not in following His Way and a refusal to bow down to His Commands, His Will. Are those who are blind equal to those who can see?

So the door was opened for That Prophet to come to show that completed Way. For how can the Messiah reign in his kingdom of the 5th Age if there is no completed Way to follow?

And the hasty say that this is wrong because they prefer not That Way as set forth by His Plan, by His Design and by His Desire. Therefore, they can make (only in their minds) another way (68).

Yet that way denies that Allah is One and in Total Control. It denies the inclusion of the one brotherhood of prophets. It denies the prophethood of Muhammad (pbh) who being only a man and no more than a man exemplifies That Way to be followed by the return of Jesus the son of Mary (pbh) (See appendix B).

In the study of comparative religion, it is always better to rely on the side of caution. For example, the knowing of religious skullduggery clearly shown throughout history does not cancel out one whit of man's responsibility to set things in order by Allah's Permission. This takes the attitude of fairness and balance into account.

In the reported sayings of Jesus, one must look at them very closely and try and understand that what he is supposed to have said has a meaning and what he said should have been reported with accuracy. However, it is true that people came and took what he said and either out of ignorance or out of criminality or even forgetfulness put some of these sayings where they did not belong – for reasons best left until Judgment Day.

Two examples of these sayings are found in Matthew (27: 46) (7) and Luke 23: 43) (8). The sayings appear to be correct but not in the way or correct place where people could understand them properly.

As to Matthew (27:46), the saying is correct but that was not said by Jesus (pbh). It was said by Simon the Cyrenian. For Jesus was accounted by his Lord as righteous, pure and perfect as Vicegerent having passed the test in obedience in faith and trust. Besides being perfect, he knew even before going to Jerusalem what was going to happen as was reported in the book, *The Non-Crucifixion of Jesus* (pbh).

Also note that Luke (23: 43) is found the promise given to that man that laid down his life on the cross for the love of God and His Messiah.

It is a well-known fact admitted by the vast majority of honest, Christian scholars that the New Testament contains 'peculiarities'. Here, in this example, we find a 'cut and paste' procedure of juggling the books as it were to alter things to 'fit' a certain corrupt philosophy.

These things can only be fought against by faith and a diligent but honest study of the records while not losing the real concept of what the Oneness of God and the beauty of the oneness of the brotherhood of prophets have meant to mankind if but men would accept it.

APPENDIX B

The following excerpts were taken from the book, *The Non-Crucifixion of Jesus*. This information concerns that 'other Semitic line' from Prophet Abraham (pbh) showing the connection between one scripture and another. The date of this manuscript called, The *Acts of the Apostles* was written probably in the late 70s of the first century or the early 80s.

And He shall send Jesus Christ {again}, which before was preached unto you (Jews):
Whom <u>the heaven must receive until the times of restitution of all things</u>, which God has spoken by the mouth of all His holy prophets since the world began.
For Moses truly said unto the fathers, a Prophet shall the Lord your God raise up unto you of <u>your brethren</u>, <u>like unto me</u>; him shall you hear <u>in all things</u> whatsoever he shall say unto you.
And it shall come to pass, that <u>every soul</u>, which will

75

not hear That Prophet, SHALL BE DESTROYED FROM AMONG THE PEOPLE. ACTS (3: 20-23).

From among 'your brethren' is an interesting piece of information. Historically, the Semitic peoples have two separate lines coming from the line of Abraham (pbh) – the line of Isaac (pbh) and the line of Ishmael (pbh). Jesus being the last of the 'Jewish prophets' is the last of the line called the Isaac line. The words 'your brethren' therefore must by all logical definition be amongst the 'other' line or the Ishmael line which is considered today as the line called the Arab line.

A few Christian notables in the past have spoken that they knew very well that another prophet would come after Jesus and that this prophet would be from the Arab line. However, these notables gave no indication that he would come from Arabia. Historically, it seems that the thought of another prophet (kept very much secret from the going concern outside the priest-class) was going to come from the land now known as Syria.

The discussion of these verses together with a few other verses in the Old and New Testament shows without ambiguity who that new and expected Prophet will be. To deny these things for any reason, except for those mentally incapacitated, is a sign of pure ignorance and contempt. It cannot be hidden from men nor will it be hidden in the heavens and there is no place to hide or to pretend a cover-up. The ONE UNIVERSAL GOD, the God of all the creation and of humankind is not duped, tricked or outmaneuvered by His created things.

Frankly speaking, Jesus (pbh) was taken up to the heavens 40 days after his Passion according to *The Acts of the Apostles*. Therefore, the Jesus that was preached to 'them' has left the earth for several decades and won't come back until his much looked for SECOND COMING. Hence, when he comes, he will not declare that religion is out of vogue but will follow a BOOK, A WAY and A PRACTICE (SUNNAH). That particular book, way and practice will come from That Prophet who was sent after him or after his first coming into the world.

Because Jesus will follow those practices already established, it becomes crystal clear that those who do not hear (CONFORM TO THOSE PRACTICES, WAY AND THAT BOOK) will be 'DESTROYED FROM AMONG THE PEOPLE.' And this thought is further enhanced from Math. (13: 41-42):

The son of man shall send forth his angels, and they shall gather <u>out of his kingdom</u> all things that offend, and them which do iniquity;
And shall cast them into a furnace of fire: there shall be wailing and gnashing of teeth. Math (13: 41-42)

People can argue that the Arabs (but they are not the majority of Muslims) have woefully neglected their religion or do not perform according to its standards. Argue away but acknowledge the Pathway. Failure to do so puts the mirror on those who desire to define themselves as 'knowers' of His Word over even Himself. And even those who do this, even if they were to bring a ransom of a mountain of gold for their souls, it would not be accepted. Why? Does the Creator Lord feel poor or frightened by any worldly power? Or is it man's arrogance that becomes his 'god' or real lover. In any case, the turning towards the Real Reality is a prime requisite for salvation and <u>not by gimmicks</u> will man be saved...

Some people might ask, "When were these thoughts concerning the coming of a new prophet lost in historic times?" It would be difficult if not impossible to come to a definitive answer. A hard look at Christian history shows several 'dark' periods where vital knowledge is missing. The best evidence so far, which is admittedly spotty, shows several things.

There is no general trend after 100 AC that is known that shows any major evidence for a strong remembrance of another Prophet to come after Jesus. It is true that there arose many different sects concerning Jesus of Nazareth. It is also true that a formalized version of 'true' Christianity did not appear until around about 130 AC. It is also true that one of Paul's favorite 'churches', the Corinthians, were one of the last to hold out for the non-crucifixion of Jesus. Finally, it is true that the formation of a real coordinated New Testament of some sorts came around 170 AC. So what can be made of this?

It would appear that through martyrdom and generation dilution, as to true knowledge of the faith, the idea of a new Prophet to arise became lost in the shuffle (out of sight, out of mind) as an important issue somewhere around 100 AC. A few sects probably held on to that idea as a major tenant of belief but because of Fitna (turmoil) spoken by Jesus, John (16: 33) caused so much trouble along with the 'wolves in sheep's clothing' or corrupt spiritual guides, the knowledge of a new Prophet became reduced to a trivial matter.

In addition, since there were no printing presses at that time, various sects were like islands in a strong sea being eroded by all sorts of foolish notions. Hence, the philosophical nonsense, which engulfed the church later, could easily bury the situation under the guise of running after the total foolishness of trying to cut open the Christ and see how many natures he had!

The declaration of Acts (3: 20-23) is important for two reasons. First, it gives testimony for those who desire salvation to take heart that the One God did not leave His 'people' who He cared for in a defenseless position. His people are not defined, as being a race or nation, but those whom He has chosen from the beginning and that knowledge is with Him alone! He is the One Who possess and owns. Nobody, no person, race or religion owns, dictates or sets limits to Him. Therefore, there is no chosen people per say but there is a chosen Way which is judged solely by Him as laid down through the institution He created – the one brotherhood of prophets. These prophets were not sent to force humanity against its will but to enlist 'helpers' and loyalists of these prophets in surrender to the One God and His Will.

The second reason clearly shows that there will be another Prophet <u>after</u> Jesus. Why must this be so?

Why should another Prophet be sent and what is his purpose? Prophets are not sent to the obedient peoples because they come to instruct, purify and teach that knowledge which is lost or twisted and bring a cleaned remembrance back to the Creator Lord as He Wills it. When, however, a special Prophet is sent to <u>all of humanity</u>, this symbolizes that humanity is to be discussed as <u>a collective whole</u>. That is, that the Last Hour is NOW and that the paradise on earth as well as the Last Day of Judgment is somewhere in the future. Moreover, being the last Prophet sent gives humanity a warning that is clear and unambiguous. It also gives people a chance to refresh and renew their commitment to their Creator Lord.

However, people who are in the grip of being 'asleep' as the New Testament declares or those who are under the spell of a corrupt priest-class (willingly or unwillingly) cannot seem to grasp the logic of these things and therefore are divided and held back from seeing the obvious. If only they took more time to study the scriptures and ask for awareness, perhaps they might come to a realization of truth and harmony between people of good faith.

But lo! What has been set in motion from the beginning of time has to be completed to separate the wheat from the chaff and to complete the restitution of all things. That is one reason the Believer is asked to pray in earnest for His Grace, Mercy and Forgiveness in sincerity. And He is going to be the Judge of who is sincere and who is only pretending to be sincere. Therefore, no one can escape His Perfect net and He will collect the 'fish' and separate them as He Decides and no one will be able to argue with Him.

A person covered in slime is as a person covered in worldly affairs. If he remembers to take a bath, so much the better for him as he goes out to meet his betters. The same holds for his soul and what that person presents to his Creator Lord. This is not done overnight but if one truly remembers Him, He will <u>not</u> forget that person.

APPENDIX C

The use of brackets { } signals my interpretation put inside some of these verses in order to clarify some meanings that may be hard to understand.

1. The similitude of Jesus before Allah is as that of Adam; He created him from dust; then said to him: "Be": and he was.
The Truth (comes) from your Lord alone; so be not of those who doubt.
Q (3: 59-60)

2. That they said (in boast), "We killed Christ Jesus the son of Mary, the messenger of Allah" – but <u>they killed him not</u>, <u>nor crucified him</u>. Only <u>a likeness</u> of that was shown

81

to them. And those who differ therein <u>are full of doubts</u>, with no (certain) knowledge but only conjecture to follow, <u>for of a surety they killed him not.</u>
Nay, Allah raised him up unto Himself; and Allah is Exalted in Power the Wise.
Q (S. 4: 157-158)

3. <u>What is with you must vanish: What is with Allah will endure.</u> And We will reward those who practice fortitude according to their best deeds. Whosoever does righteous deeds, whether male or female, provided he is a believer, We will certainly grant him <u>to live a pure life in this world and We will reward such people (in the Hereafter) according to their best deeds.</u> Q (16: 96-97)

4. 'Abdullah b. Salam said the description of Moses is written in the Torah and also that <u>Jesus son of Mary will be buried along with him (Muhammad).</u> Abu Maudud said that a place for a grave has remained in the house (where Muhammad is buried)."
(Tirmidhi transmitted it.)

5. Abdullah b. 'Amr reported God's Messenger as saying, "Jesus the son of Mary will descend to the earth, will marry, have children and remain forty-five years, after which he will die and be buried along with me in my grave. Then Jesus the son of Mary and I shall arise from one grave between Abu Bakr and 'Umar."
(Ibn al-Jauzi transmitted it in Kitab al-wafa').

6. And as it is appointed unto men <u>once to die</u>, but after this the Judgment.
Heb (9: 27)

7. ... "My God, my God, why have You forsaken me?" Matt. (27: 46)

8. And Jesus said unto him, Verily I say unto you, "Today you shall be with me in paradise."
Luke (23: 43)

9. We did indeed offer <u>the Trust</u> to the heavens and the Earth and the mountains; but they refused to undertake it, being afraid thereof: <u>but man undertook it: he was indeed unjust and foolish.</u>
Q (33: 72)

10. The Kursi mentioned in Q (2: 255) is completely different than the Throne of Allah. Prophet Muhammad (pbh) said: "The Kursi compared to the Throne ('Arsh) is nothing but <u>like a ring</u> thrown out upon open space of the desert." Imagine, if you will, <u>that if the Kursi extends over the complete, expanding universe, then how much greater is the Throne!</u>

11. <u>He cannot be questioned</u> for His acts, but they will be questioned (for theirs).
Q (21:23)

12. Anas reported God's messenger as saying, "When God fashioned Adam in paradise He left him as long as God wished to leave him; then Iblis began to visit him and consider what kind of being he was, and when he saw that he had a hollow space within <u>he recognized that he had been created as a being not possessed of self-control.</u>"
(Muslim transmitted it)

13. "<u>Was he (Adam) worthy</u> of this {the Angels prostrated

before Adam to show their submission to their Lord's Will and to show their inferiority to The Man} <u>that You have exalted him over me? If You give me respite</u> up to the Day of Resurrection, I will uproot the whole of his progeny: there shall only be a few of them who will be able to save themselves from me."
Q (17: 62)

14. It is such as obey Allah and His Messenger, and fear Allah and do right, that will triumph.
Q (24: 52)

15. It is He, Who made <u>you the vicegerents on the earth</u> and raised some of you above others in ranks <u>so that He may test you</u> in what He has given you. Indeed, your Lord is swift in inflicting punishment yet He is also very Forgiving and Merciful. Q (6: 165)

16. <u>He it is Who made you vicegerents in the earth. Now, whoever disbelieves shall himself bear the burden of disbelief</u> ... Q (35: 39)

17. Those who reject faith and deny Our Signs will be companions of the Hell-fire. Q (5: 10)

18. This is because of the (unrighteous deeds) which your hands sent on before you: for Allah never does injustice to those who serve Him. Q (3: 182)

19. "This Our Record speaks about you with truth: for We were wont to put on record all that you did." Q (45: 27-29)

20. And remember that Abraham was <u>tried by his Lord with certain commands, which he fulfilled</u>: He said: "I will make

you an Imam to the people. He pleaded: "And also (Imams) from my offspring!" He answered: "But My Promise is not within the reach of evil-doers."
Q (2: 124)

21. Jabir reported God's messenger as saying, "The prophets were presented before me and I saw Moses of a type which resembled one of the men of Shanu'a. I saw Jesus son of Mary, and the nearest to him in appearance whom I have seen is 'Urwa b. Mas'ud. I saw Abraham, and <u>the nearest to him in appearance whom I have seen is your companion (meaning himself)</u>. I also saw Gabriel, and the nearest to him in appearance whom I have seen is Dihya b. Khalifa." (Muslim transmitted it).

22. Wathila b. al-Asqa' told that he heard God's messenger say, "God chose Kinana from the descendants of Ishmael. He chose Quraish from Kinana. From Quraish, He chose the B. Hashim, and He chose me from the B. Hashim." Muslim transmitted it. In a version by Tirmidhi he said, "<u>God chose Ishmael from among the children of Abraham</u>, and He chose the B. Kinana from among the descendents of Ishmael."

23. Al-'Irbad b. Sariya reported God's messenger as saying, "I was inscribed in God's presence as the seal of the prophets <u>when Adam was prone in his basic substance</u>. I shall inform you about the <u>beginning of my career: it was the petition of Abraham, the Good Tidings by Jesus</u>, and the vision my mother saw when she gave birth to me and a light issued to her from which the castles of Syria shone for her." (It is transmitted in Sharh as-sunna, and Ahmad transmitted it on the authority of Abu Umama from "I shall inform you … to the end.)

24. <u>Never think that Allah would fail His Messengers in His Promise</u>: For Allah is Exalted in Power – The Lord of Retribution. Q (14: 47)

25. Those who strive against Our Signs, to frustrate them, will be given over into Chastisement.
Q (34: 38)

26. How much more should the blood of Christ, who through the eternal Spirit offered himself <u>without spot</u> to God, purge your conscience from dead works to serve the Living God?
Heb. (9: 14)

27. He shall glorify me: <u>for he {Prophet Muhammad} shall receive of mine</u>, and shall show it unto you.
John (16: 14)

28. Therefore will I divide him {the Messiah} a portion with the great and he shall divide the spoil with the strong {in the kingdom given to him}; <u>because he has poured out his soul unto death</u>: he was numbered with the transgressors; and he bare the sin of many, and made intercession for the transgressors. Isaiah (53: 12)

29. Verily this is no less than a Message to (all) the worlds ... Q (81: 27)

30. It is reported on the authority of Talha b. 'Ubaidullah that a person with disheveled hair, one of the people of Nejd, came to the Messenger of Allah (may peace be upon him). We heard the humming of his voice, but could not fully discern what he had been saying, till he came nigh to the Messenger of Allah (may peace be upon him). It

was then (disclosed to us) that he was asking questions pertaining to Islam. The Messenger of Allah (may peace be upon him) said: Five prayers during the day and the night. (Upon this) he said: Am I obliged to say any other (prayer) besides these? He (the Holy Prophet) said: No, but whatever you observe voluntarily, out of your own free will, and the fasts of Ramadan. The inquirer said: Am I obliged to do anything else besides this? He (the Holy Prophet) said: No, but whatever you do out of your own free will. And the Messenger of Allah told him about the Zakat (poor-rate). The inquirer said: Am I obliged to pay anything else besides this? He (the Holy Prophet) said: No, but whatever you pay voluntarily out of your own free will. The man turned back and was saying: <u>I would neither make any addition to this, nor will I decrease anything out of it.</u> The Prophet remarked: <u>He is successful,</u> {that is he would enter heaven (Paradise) if he were true to his profession} <u>if he is true to what he affirms.</u> (Sahih Muslim)

31. Abu Musa reported the Prophet as saying, "<u>Many men have been perfect,</u> but among women only Mary the daughter of 'Imran and Asiya the wife of Pharaoh were perfect; and 'A'isha's superiority over women is like the superiority of tharid over other kinds of food." (Bukhari and Muslim)

32. I and my Father are one. John (10: 30)

33. Narrated Abu Hurairah: The Prophet said, "Allah says, I am just as My slave thinks I am, (i.e. <u>I am able to do for him what he thinks I can do for him) and I am with him if he remembers Me.</u> If he remembers Me in himself, I too, remember him in Myself; and if he remembers Me in a group of people, I remember him in a group that is better

than them; and if he comes one span nearer to Me, I go one cubit nearer to him; and if he comes one cubit nearer to Me, I go a distance of two outstretched arms nearer to him; and if he comes to Me walking, I go to him running."
(Sahih Al-Bukhari)

34. Abu Hurairah reported Allah's Messenger (may peace by upon him) as saying: The satan touches every son of Adam on the day when his mother gives birth to him with the exception of Mary and her son. (Sahih Muslim)

35. Who needs not daily, as those {regular} high priests, to offer up a sacrifice, first for his own sins, {shortcomings/ imperfections} and then for the people's: for this he did once, when he offered up himself {to be that Sign or Sacrifice}. Heb. (7: 27)

36. Though he were a Son, yet learned he obedience by the things which he suffered;
And being made perfect, he became the author of eternal salvation unto all them who obey Him {God}. Heb. (5: 8-9)

37. For it is not possible that the blood of bulls and of goats should take away sins.
Wherefore when he cometh into the world, he said {concerning God}, Sacrifice and offering You would not, but a BODY hast Thou (O God) prepared (for) me:
In burnt offerings and sacrifices for sin You have had no pleasure.
Then said I, Lo, I come (in the volume of the book it is written of me,) to do Your Will, O God. Heb. (10: 4-7)

38. And for this cause {because he offered himself without spot as to be sinless} he is the mediator of the new testament

{new law – that which will come (Islam) and that which he shall inherit in the 5th Age}, that by means of death, for the redemption of transgressions that were under the first testament {the old law – The Law of Retribution – cause and effect} they which are called {unto the Way} might receive the promise of eternal inheritance {under the new law – as to his kingdom given to him in the 5th Age upon his return}.

For where a testament is {paradigm change}, there must also of necessity be the {some form of} death of the testator. Heb. (9: 15-16)

39. For since by man {Adam} came death, {following after him {Adam} in pattern by our own actions} by man {the Christ} came also the resurrection of the dead {not led or taught by Angels out into the Light but through a man}.

For as in Adam all die {as the pattern has been set each according his own strivings}, even so in Christ shall all be made alive {as the pattern has been set each according to his own strivings (*61)}.

I Cor. (15: 21-22)

40. Abu Hurairah reported God's messenger as saying, "The way in which I may be compared with the prophets is by a castle which was beautifully constructed, but in which the place of one brick was left incomplete. Sightseers went round admiring the beauty of its construction with the exception of the place for that brick. Now I have filled up the place of that brick, in me the building is complete and in me the messengers are complete." (Bukhari and Muslim)

41. For this is the Covenant that I will make with the House of Israel {servants of Allah}. After those days, said the Lord, I will put My laws into their mind, and write them in their

hearts: and I will be to them a God and they shall be to Me a people – {in the 5ᵗʰ Age to come or that kingdom the Messiah will inherit}
And they shall not teach every man his neighbor, and every man his brother, saying, know the Lord: for all shall know Me, from the least to the greatest.
For I will be Merciful to their unrighteousness and their sins and their iniquities will I remember no more {in that kingdom of the 5ᵗʰ Age (*3, 72)}.
In that He says, a new covenant {by which} He (God) has made the first old. Now that which decays and waxes old is ready to vanish away {hence the 5ᵗʰ Age of man to come – (*64)}. Heb (8: 10-13)

42. Behold! The angels said, "O Mary! Allah gives you glad tidings of a Word from Him: his name will be Christ Jesus, the son of Mary, held in honor in this world and the Hereafter and of (the company of) those nearest to Allah." Q (3: 45)

43. And why behold you the mote that is in your brother's eye, but consider not the beam that is in your own eye?
Or how will you say to your brother, "Let me pull out the mote out of your eye; and, behold, and a beam is in your own eye?
You hypocrite, first cast out the beam out of your own eye; then shall you see clearly to cast out the mote out of your brother's eye. Math (7: 3-5)

44. And We made the son of Mary as a Sign ... Q (23: 50)

45. And he (Satan) brought him to Jerusalem, and set him on a pinnacle of the temple, and said unto him, if you are the (Son of God) {Messiah}, cast yourself down from hence:

For it is written, <u>He shall give His Angels charge over thee, to keep thee (safe)</u>:
And in their hands <u>they shall bear thee up, lest at any time you would dash your foot against a stone</u>. Luke (4: 9-12)

46. Jesus therefore, <u>knowing all the things that should come upon him</u>, went forth, and said unto them, who do you seek? John (18: 4)

47. All who obey Allah and the Messenger are in the company of those on whom is the Grace of Allah, of the Prophets (who teach), the sincere (lovers of truth), the martyrs, and the righteous (who do good): Ah! How beautiful is their company.
Such is the Bounty from Allah: and sufficient is it that Allah knows all (things).
Q (4: 69-70)

48. Abu Hurairah reported God's messenger as saying, "<u>I am the nearest of kin to Jesus son of Mary in this world and the next</u>. The prophets are brothers, sons of one father by co-wives. Their mothers are different, but <u>their religion is one</u>. <u>There has been no prophet between us</u>."
(Bukhari and Muslim)

49. And thus have We, by Our command, sent Inspiration to you: <u>you did not know</u> (before) what was Revelation, and what was Faith; but We have made the (Quran) a Light, wherewith We guide such of Our servants as We will; and verily you do guide (men) to the Straight Way. Q (42: 52)

50. Praise be to Allah, Who has sent to His Servant The Book and has allowed NO crookedness therein. Q (18: 1)

51. Had We sent down this Quran on a mountain, verily, you would have seen it <u>humble itself and cleave asunder for fear of Allah</u>. Such are the similitudes which We propound to men, <u>that they may reflect</u>. Q (59: 21)

52. 'Aisha reported that Harith b. Hisham asked Allah's Apostle (pbh), "How does the wahi (Revelation) come to you? He said, "At times it comes to me like the ringing of a bell and that is most severe for me and when it is over I retain that (what I had received in the form of wahi), and at times an Angel in the form of a human being comes to me (and speaks) and I retain whatever he speaks. (Muslim)

53. Anas told that Gabriel came to God's messenger when he was playing with some other boys, seized him, threw him down, split open his heart and took out of it a clot of blood, saying, "<u>This is the devil's portion in you</u>." He then washed it with Zamzam water in a gold dish, repaired it, and put it back in its place. The boys went running to his mother, i.e. his foster -mother, saying, "Muhammad has been killed," so they went to him and found him looking upset. Anas said he used to see the mark of the sewing in his breast. (Muslim transmitted it.)

54. And Jesus said, "somebody has touched me: for I perceive virtue has gone out of me."
And when the woman saw that she was not hid, she came trembling, and falling down before him, she declared unto him before all the people for what cause she had touched him, and how she was healed immediately. Luke (8: 46-47)

55. Jubair b. Mutim told that he heard the Prophet say, "I have names. I am Muhammad, I am Ahmad, I am al-Mahi (the obliterator) by whom God obliterates infidelity, I am

al-Hashir (the gatherer) who will gather mankind at my feet (*57), I am al-Aqib (the last in succession), al-Aqib being <u>the one after whom will be no prophet</u>." (Bukhari and Muslim)

56. Abu Hurairah reported God's messenger as saying, "I have been given superiority over the prophets in six respects: <u>I have been given words which are concise but comprehensive in meaning</u>; I have been helped by terror (in the hearts of enemies); spoils have been made lawful to me; the earth has been made for me a place of worship and ceremonially pure; <u>I have been sent to all mankind</u>; and <u>the line of prophets is closed with me</u>. (Muslim)

57. Abu Hurairah in a lengthy hadith reported: Meat was one day brought to the Messenger of Allah (pbh) and a foreleg was offered to him, a part which he liked ... and said, "I shall be the leader of mankind on the Day of Resurrection. Do you know why? Allah would gather in one plain the earlier and the later (of the human race) on the Day of Resurrection. Then the voice of the proclaimer would be heard by all of them and the eyesight would penetrate through all of them and the sun would come near. People would then experience a degree of <u>anguish, anxiety and agony which they shall not be able to bear</u> and they shall not be able to stand. Some people would say to the others, "Go to Adam." And they would go to Adam and say, "O Adam, you are the father of mankind. Allah created you by His own Hand and breathed into you of His spirit and ordered the Angels to prostrate before you. Intercede for us with your Lord. Don't you see what (trouble) we are facing? Don't you see what (misfortune) has overtaken us? Adam would say, "Verily, my Lord is angry to an extent to which He had never been angry before nor

would He be angry afterward. Verily, He forbade me (to go near) that tree and I disobeyed Him. I am concerned with my own self. Go to someone else; go to Noah… {The rest of the hadith follows this same pattern – from Noah to Abraham to Moses and then comes Jesus} They would come to Jesus and would say, "O Jesus, you are the messenger of Allah and you conversed with people in the cradle, (you are) His Word which He sent down upon Mary, and (you are) the Spirit from Him; so intercede for us with your Lord. Don't you see (the trouble) in which we are? Don't you see (the misfortune) that has overtaken us? Jesus (pbh) would say, "Verily, my Lord is angry today as He had never been angry before or would ever be angry afterwards." He (then continued) but mentioned no sin of his. (He simply said) "I am concerned with myself, I am concerned with myself; you go to someone else: better go to Muhammad (pbh)." The people would come to me and say, "O Muhammad, you are the Messenger of Allah and the last of the prophets. Allah has pardoned all of your previous and later sins. Intercede for us with your Lord; don't you see in which (trouble) we are? Don't you see what (misfortune) has overtaken us?" I shall then set off and come below the Throne and fall down prostrate before my Lord; then Allah would reveal to me and inspire me with some of His Praises and Glorifications which He had not revealed to anyone before me. He would then say, "Muhammad, raise your head; ask and it would be granted; intercede and intercession would be accepted." I would then raise my head and say, "O my Lord, my people, my people." It would be said, "O Muhammad, bring in by the right gate of Paradise those of your people who would have no account to render. They would share with the people some other door besides this door. The Holy Prophet then said, "By Him in Whose Hand is the life of Muhammad, verily the distance between two door leaves of the Paradise is as great as between Makkah and Hajar, or as between Makkah and Busra." (Muslim)

58. 'Umar reported God's Messenger as saying, "Do not eulogize me as the Christians eulogized the son of Mary. I am just His servant, so say, 'God's servant and Messenger.'" (Bukhari and Muslim)

59. Abu Hurairah reported God's Messenger as saying, "It is not fitting for a man to say I am better than Jonah son of Matta." (Bukhari and Muslim)

60. These things I have spoken unto you that in me you might have peace. In the world you shall have tribulation; but be of good cheer; I have overcome the world. John (16: 33)

61. Who receives guidance receives it for his own benefit: who goes astray does so to his own loss: No bearer of burdens can bear the burden of another: Q (17: 15)

62. Man prays for evil {earnest desirous thoughts/wishes} as fervently as he prays {earnest desirous thoughts/wishes} for good for man is given to haste.
Q (17: 11)

63. Abu Hurairah reported the Prophet as telling that when God created paradise He said to Gabriel, "Go and look at it." He went and looked at it and at what God had prepared in it for its inhabitants, then came and said, "O my Lord, by Thy Might, no one who hears of it will fail to enter it." He then surrounded it with disagreeable things and said, "Go and look at it, Gabriel." He went and looked at it, then came and said, "O my Lord, by Thy Might, I am afraid that no one will enter it." When God created hell He said, "Go

and look at it, Gabriel." He went and looked at it, then came and said, "O my Lord, by Thy Might, no one who hears of it will enter it." He then surrounded it with <u>desirable things</u> and said, "Go and look at it, Gabriel." He went and looked at it, then said, "O my Lord, by Thy Might, I am afraid that no one will remain who does not enter it."
Tirmidhi, Abu Dawud and Nasa'i transmitted it.

64. Therefore, I say unto you, <u>the kingdom of God shall be taken away from you, and given to a nation</u> <u>bringing forth the fruits thereof</u> {through its purified way/instruction}. Matt. (21: 43)

65. "I have come to you to attest the Torah which was before me. And to make lawful to you part of what was (before) forbidden to you; I have come to you with a Sign from your Lord. So fear Allah and obey me." Q (3: 50)

66. <u>Do they seek for other than the Religion of Allah</u> – while all creatures in the heavens and on the earth have, <u>willingly or unwillingly,</u> bowed to His Will (accepted Islam) and to Him shall they all be brought back? Q (3:83)

67. It is He Who has sent His Messenger with Guidance and the religion of truth to cause it to prevail over all religion, even though the pagans may detest (it).
Q (9: 33)

68. Verily, verily, I say unto you, He that enters not by the door into the sheepfold, <u>but climbs up some other way,</u> the same is a thief and a robber. John (10: 1)

69. Narrated Ibn 'Abbas: The Prophet said: "Allah said, "The son of Adam tells lies against Me though he has no right to

do so, and he abuses Me though he has no right to do so. As for his telling lies against Me, he claims that I cannot re-create him as I created him before; <u>and as for his abusing Me: it is his statement that I have a son (or offspring) No! Glorified is Me! I am far from taking a wife or a son (or offspring)</u>." (Sahih Al-Bukhari)

70. Abu Hurairah reported Allah's Messenger (pbh) as saying: "Observe moderation in deeds (and if it is not possible, try to be near moderation) and understand that <u>none amongst you can attain salvation because of his deeds alone</u>." They said: "Allah's Messenger, not even you?" Thereupon he said: "<u>Not even me</u>, but that Allah should wrap me in His Mercy and Grace."

71. Give not that which is holy unto the dogs, and do not cast your pearls before swine, lest they trample them under their feet, and turn again and rend you. Matt (7: 6)

72. And there is none of the People of the Book but <u>must believe in him</u> {Jesus} {follow him in – his practices of Islam and the Prophet's Sunnah upon his return} <u>before his death</u> (6); and on the Day of Judgment <u>he will be a witness against them</u>. Q (4: 159)
This verse should be further explained in more detail by observing appendix B which talks about this subject in further detail. It must be remembered that those, whose agenda is to destroy the truth, at times seem mighty. They only pile up for themselves humiliation upon humiliation. So, let those who have faith; let them have faith and let those who wish to quibble; let them quibble. See how their pet theories of self-glorification and magic will protect them on that most terrible of Days when all souls will be under unimaginable stress.

**73. For then will I turn to the people a <u>pure language</u> {a religious language} that they may all call upon the name of the Lord, to serve him with one consent {standing shoulder to shoulder}.
From beyond the rivers of Ethiopia {Arabia}, my suppliants, even the daughter of my dispersed {Semitic line from Ishmael}, shall bring My offering.
Zephaniah (3: 9-10)**

Granted the world in its present form is often on a hectic and confusing pace. The same might be said for those who try and study religion. Of course there are the good people and the people whose agenda behind doing these things are not good. Such is the way with the world and those who live in it.

One would think that the simple declaration concerning 'there is only ONE GOD' would be a simple matter and a joyful thought amongst the believers. But look closely at the so-called defenders of the faith and truth (any particular faith) and one can see that some people have their own minds about this matter and would prefer self-gratification than truthful research – at least some of the time. A simple coming together of the minds in peace and harmony sounds simple but the 'human factor' makes it overly complex.

The basis for what man calls religion is for SALVATION and <u>human guidance</u> as well as the understanding of who we are, where we came from and the duties we owe to our Creator Lord. Is that so difficult to understand? Logically, it is not difficult but in practicality it appears daunting. And we have been given certain 'keys' to help us seek out a proper understanding. But many people refuse this notion because they want some sort of glorification of the self and that raises friction between certain groups – hence the idea of envy/jealousy/pride being allowed to darken the 'light' of understanding.

When the light of understanding (Universal Logic) is allowed to penetrate the soul, it is not becoming of one to go around blaming the One God but rather seeing the corruption in the self. And ALL have that certain corruption but to various degrees from minor to major. Hence, for those who can see, let them see and in nowise are the blind equal to those who can see. It doesn't take a mystic (of whom I simply mistrust for the most part) nor does it take a genius to figure out what is going on in some so-called religious circles. However, that is life and that is that!

Let me, as Allah Wills, address some issues to help avoid confusion. In knowing that reading all of my seven books, which I hardly expect people to do, there must come about some misunderstandings because some concepts are hard to understand. Imagine what happens when someone reads only one book out of the seven. Where is the train of thought going to lead? That is the problem. So, as Allah Wills, I want to start off with a kind of review.

The first principle in religion is that there is, has been and will only ever be but ONE GOD. He is the ONE Who has no partners, peers or relations and He is so far above any of His creations that the minds of the best of peoples (Abraham, Moses, Jesus and Muhammad – peace be upon them all – cannot fathom His complete Greatness or Essence. They felt it deep within side their souls but as to containing that Greatness none of the creation, even if it was stacked altogether to take a part of that understanding, could ever hope to achieve the sum total of THE GOD!

The next thing is that He, out of His Mercy and Kindness, elevates those of His creation as He chooses and provides support and guidance unto His creations so that they will be reinforced spiritually and guided rightly – as they so choose. For it is up to those who are of the dominate groups (those having free will) to choose between His Way or their way. This in no way declares that, for example, man has to break his head to become perfect but that he must follow the pathway that acknowledges His Greatness plus a willful attempt at enduring the many trials of life to become obedient unto Him. And because of His Greatness, He showered man with an easier road by sending not Angels but other men of high and excellent quality to be followed and obeyed as much as one could. Hence, the brotherhood of prophets came into being.

All of the prophets gave understanding to the BASICS needed for the final goal to be obtained which is SALVATION. And this salvation is based on Trusting in the Creator Lord – the One God. And over one-hundred thousand prophets came to refresh this belief to mankind so that no person would be left behind – unless of course one chose another route. And even if one chose 'evil' and <u>insisted on it</u>, that person would still be rewarded by negative growth for the ONE GOD is not unjust.

However, enough said about that. The important thing is that there is a one brotherhood of prophets who served THE ONE GOD in harmony and unity having the same goal in mind – Salvation.

Not only do we speak of the One God but now we speak of the one brotherhood of prophets. The one brotherhood of prophets is a body of the highest believers who are <u>in agreement with each other and who do not form contradictory pathways for salvation</u>. And with a few of these 'higher' prophets came 'Books' declaring the harmony and oneness of what man calls religion but more specifically called THE WAY, meaning HIS WAY. This 'road map' to The Way was to act as a guide to those groups of people given it. However, what does true history tell us about how <u>these prophets were treated</u>? So, when that certain prophet died, how would one expect the books that they brought, as in knowledge that they contained, would be treated?

Some of mankind are criminally abusive and want to breakup UNITY by either altering the proven WORD or by twisting it verbally as to bend THE WAY into their way being likened to fancy flights of fiction. But even thus, the records still retain the flavor of harmony and unity. So the records, especially those records taken from those who are called 'People of the Book' as they are so honored because they retained <u>the more purified way</u>, ARE ONE!

So far we have the ONE GOD, the One brotherhood of prophets, the One Way and the Oneness of the records. But we still have the oneness of mankind to deal with.

In the beginning, of which we hardly know anything about, mankind was ONE NATION. It wasn't the One God that scattered the people to and fro but it was on their heads that caused the separation. Like their father Adam (pbh) they did manage to wander off the pathway and it is <u>no blame on him</u> for what they did. However, the One God knew about these things and He provided those pathways for the so called 'superior set' (mankind) to find out just how dependent they were on Him. But that is another story and He alone knows the full truth about that.

The whole concept of any true religion is to submit to His Divine Will in bowing down to His Way and that may confuse some who falsely are led into believing that their way is His Way. Just by going to the basics shows how wrong those people are. That is where the saying of one being 'full of themselves' comes in. They haven't understood the practice of the ways and actions of obedience called Sunnah of their Spiritual Leader (prophet) in their heart and therefore even if they follow something religiously, it counts for nothing because if the heart is corrupt the deeds that they do will be corrupt and likened to nothing. Hence, there is the description in the Quran of some peoples' 'good' deeds being turned into dust and rejected (Arab or non-Arab).

However that may be, human beings are not the ones to decide these matters or act as stand-ins for the One God and His Perfect Judgment. Allah is not in need of man's so-called brilliant deductions. Yet see how man operates with his logic by vindicating himself so as to gain advantage over others! An example of this can be taken from the story of how the idea of the 'sons of God' started.

What is the story about how the idea of the sons of God got started? Some people like to fashion their fanciful notions after others by blending truth with paganism or mixing the leaven with the lump.

The story from the records of the People of the Book is clear enough. Allah is known as THE LIGHT and those who follow (practice, keep in their hearts) this LIGHT are those who are on the straight path or the believers in The Way. The Way is the pathway of light and forms groups of people down through the ages as people of the light or The Way. So, they became known as children of the light or sons of the light meaning sons belonging to that group of the right guided way as opposed to the sons or children of darkness or those who are opposed to The Way or those who favor living in contrast to The Way.

The corruption now becomes easier to see. According to some faulty logic used by the deformed in heart some would say that if God is the Light, then sons of light would become sons of God.

What absolute rubbish they brought with them! This would destroy the unity of the scriptures which DEMANDS THAT PEOPLE MAKE NO PARTNERS WITH THE ONE GOD. In truth, God has no partners and that means no sons, daughters, cousins, uncles or whatever! How some have become deluded by their own so-called attractive dispositions or selfish desires by making their prophets or as in the past some good people into gods as opposed to the worship of the ONE GOD. Usually, this starts out as a supposed form of worship (the devil is a clever enemy to man) but then breaks down into self pampering notions of how superior this creed is compared with others.

Some may argue that in my books there are many contradictions. That I don't mind because being a mere reporter and a simple carbon-based life form, it is natural that contradictions might arise. However, if the term contradictions are used by some who fail to understand, then the complaint is not a valid one. For example, I do not understand anything about differential equations although I am good at arithmetic. Should I disavow the existence of differential equations then?

Comparative religion is as much as an art as a science and one must be aware to be aware. In one of my books I discussed a famous hadith by Prophet Muhammad (pbh) stating that Allah has kept for Himself five things that He alone knows. One of these things is the sex of the child before its birth – as to the soul when it is sent down is the more correct idea than at the start of conception. But mischievous people and some orientalists no doubt will latch onto the fact that scientists can now be over 99.9% certain of what sex the child will be 'before' conception.

Well that is true enough with genetic manipulation. However, these people are missing the point entirely! Talk about being misled by such shallow logic. In my book, *The Non-Crucifixion of Jesus* p. 137, I discussed the soul as to its not being able to be destroyed by any natural force in the universe and this connects to the fact that the 'spiritual' is of a higher nature than the vessel (body) holding it.

A look into the agonies of some tormented souls born into a male/female body but craving under extreme sadness and deprivation to be of the opposite sex should tell us something. The sex of the child physically can be determined by the sexual organs it has but what of the sex of the soul? That cannot be determined by any but the One God. Mysteries abound in life and it is not for us to fall into shallow disputes about matters not under our control but to observe the ways of that pathway shown to be beneficial for salvation.

To me the most beautiful story that the world has seen is the story of the Messiah-soul. To be sure, as the great prophet Isaiah (pbh) declared, Isaiah (53: 8-10) 'it pleased God to bruise him' – the Messiah soul. And if that sounds miraculous, then note that Gen. (6: 1-5) sounds just as miraculous.

But the most complete package that the world has ever known for SALVATION came in the human being known as Muhammad (pbh). He is the one whom the Messiah will follow both in this world (Quran and Sunnah) and in the Hereafter as it is given to Muhammad (pbh) to carry the banner of Praise for his Creator Lord. However, real faith is not centered around mysteries but on a solid handhold to the tenets and the desire to follow these tenets in the heart.

Others have come to claim special rights and privileges due to ignorance and folly. Ignorance which represents the people who are carelessly swindled into wrong beliefs and folly which represents those who seek for a joyous afterlife by passing on falsehoods are examples of their representative collective wholes. For example, many are under the impression that Moses (pbh) was a Jew or was connected to Judaism. In fact, Judaism started around 400 BC and that was after Moses so how is it possible that Moses (pbh) would be considered a Jew? Many may not think that this is right. So, go and find real history to find the real facts instead of being led by false assumptions.

Let the followers of Moses (pbh) take heed. He was not a Jew but rather he was a follower of The Way and let those who claim Moses (pbh) as their own let them be vigilant in understanding Deut. (18: 18-19). Let the followers of Jesus (pbh) take heed. He was not a Christian but rather he was a follower of The Way and let those who claim Jesus as their own let them be vigilant in understanding John (16: 13-14) and Acts (3: 20-23).